D0635482

DD	DV	BB	BR
1119			
DL	DW	BD	BT
DM	DX	BM	BV

To my beautiful boys.
I hope the world stays
green for you.

First published in the UK in 2009
by Collins & Brown
10 Southcombe Street
London W14 0RA

An imprint of Anova Books Company Ltd

ISBN 978-1-84340-492-7

A CIP catalogue for this book is available
from the British Library.

10 9 8 7 6 5 4 3 2 1

Reproduction by Mission Productions,
Hong Kong

Printed and bound by 1010 Printing
International Ltd, China

This book can be ordered direct from the
publisher at www.anovabooks.com.

With regard to
managing the
world's resources,
Ghandi once said:
'There is enough in
the world for
everybody's need,
but not enough for
everybody's greed!'

CONTENTS

Introduction 4

GREEN HOME IMPROVEMENTS

Why go Green?............................12

Basic Building Materials 15

Windows and Doors 45

Green Insulation 53

FIXTURES AND FITTINGS

Essential Elements......................72

Green Appliances 92

POWERING THE HOME

Energy Reserves.......................114

Sustainable Energy Sources......120

Heating 128

Water 144

THE GREEN OUTDOORS

Be Eco-friendly Outdoors 156

Roofs..176

Glossary 184

Directory 186

Index 190

Acknowledgements 192

INTRODUCTION

Climate change is a huge issue. Variations in climate do happen over time, but what we have seen in recent decades, is that human activity is believed to be causing the planet to heat up faster than it would naturally. The Earth's atmosphere is protected from extremes of temperature by a layer of gases known as the ozone layer. However, since the Industrial Revolution (1760–1850) 'greenhouse gases', which include carbon dioxide, methane and nitrous oxide have increased in volume and caused the Earth's temperature to increase more quickly than it would naturally.

In the UK this has manifested itself in higher temperatures in summer; there is less snow in winter, flash flooding is becoming increasingly common, and storms and rising sea levels mean our coastline is under threat.

Most of us do care about the environment, but given the scale of the problem, it is difficult to see how what we do as individuals and homeowners can make a difference. One startling statistic may help – did you know more than 25 per cent of the carbon dioxide, the main greenhouse gas that causes climate change, produced in the UK comes from houses and flats?

Taking a wider view though, going 'green' really is a minefield. It seems fairly widely accepted that the way we are treating the environment and ourselves is at best not brilliant and at worst a disaster, and most of us really want to do better. But – and it's a big but – which is the right way to go? Faced with the 'buy organic, foreign beans from the specialist food shop or non-organic, own-brand beans from your favourite supermarket' dilemma – which way do you go? Should you dash out and buy a wind turbine, and

SOURCE QUOTE: ENERGY SAVING TRUST

spend the weekend up a ladder trying to screw it to your chimney stack, or are you in fact just fuelling the consumer nonsense that has got us into this parlous plight in the first place?

> In 2006, total UK CO_2 emissions were almost 555 million tonnes.

What I would like is a balanced and rational view on green issues in the home. It seems that one day you read one thing, and the next you read something that contradicts it entirely. Also, it would be good to have answers to some really obvious questions that no-one seems to ask, such as: why, when we live on an island surrounded by water and where it always rains, do we need to save water? Low energy light bulbs may make sense in theory, but as they take so long to warm up do you now leave all the lights in the house on in the evening, rather than just having them on in the room you are sitting in?

Without question, in life the 'greenest' thing to do is less – spend less, travel less, consume less, change less and heat less. But I think there has to be a healthy dose of realism with everything. We can make a commitment to live greener lives without having to radically change our lifestyles.

Our lives are considerably easier now that we are not hand-washing our clothes and squeezing out the water by running them through a mangle. However the end result of this domestic simplicity is that we have now got rather used to our clothes being pretty close to clean, and I can't believe I am the only parent who turns a conspicuously blind eye to their children covering their T-shirts in cake mixture, knowing that they can be washed with the push of a button. And we all have to admit it is nice to have a warm

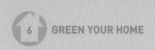

house and every modern convenience. Even the man-made chemicals that we are surrounded by in everything we use often make products work better and last longer.

So can we find a balance? Can we do less and use less without inconveniencing our lives too much? And if we want to do more, then how do we go about it? It makes sense that if we want our houses to be warm then we should try to keep as much heat in as possible. And if we want a cup of tea, then why not use a kettle that uses the least amount of electricity, and only use as much water as we need?

There are three ways we can make our homes more 'green'. First, we can improve the green credentials of our property, for example in the way we conserve energy, produce our electricity, dispose of our waste, or use less water. Second, we can go about more conventional home improvements – such as repainting our living room, or reflooring the bathroom – using greener materials. Third, we can make our buying decisions more carefully. If we want to upgrade our fridge, do we pay the council to take away the old one, or do we find out if someone else can make use of it?

Green Your Home is divided into four sections. The first, **Green Home Improvements**, looks at the choice of materials available for completing jobs around the home, and explains why some are greener than others. It also looks at how to improve insulation throughout your home – roofs, walls, floors and tanks and pipes – and introduces the very latest, green insulating materials.

" The volume of waste produced in the UK in one hour would fill the Albert Hall. "

SOURCE QUOTE: SCOTTISH ENVIRONMENT PROTECTION AGENCY

Fixtures and Fittings starts by looking at the kitchen and bathroom – the two rooms in the house that use the most energy and have the most scope for becoming greener. This section also looks at lighting, water heating and appliances, explaining the range of products available and highlighting which ones represent the greenest choice.

Powering the Home tackles the big projects: electricity generation, heating and water conservation. It is these changes that start to take a home down the road towards true sustainability – the dream of every eco-warrior. However, with rising fuel and electricity prices such changes may begin to represent a realistic financial option for increasing numbers of us.

The final section, **The Green Outdoors** concentrates on our outside space; how we can make our gardens greener in more ways than one: by reusing water, installing a green roof on our shed, or using permeable materials when laying a patio or off-street parking to help avoid flash-flooding.

The aim of this book is to outline how you can make your home greener in a way that suits your lifestyle and your budget. As I have mentioned before it is also about being realistic: we can't make many changes all at once, and we can't make all the changes that are available, but when we do make them we can be more informed and perhaps make our decisions in a greener way.

Sarah Beeny
September 2009

 CARBON CUTTING

Green Your Home addresses both aspects of our carbon footprint: finding the most appropriate energy-saving improvements for our homes, and selecting the right type of materials, and then offers clear cost comparisons for the options available so that you can make an informed choice.

CARBON FOOTPRINT

This is a calculation that represents the impact your home and activities have on the environment, and in particular on climate change. It is a measurement of all greenhouse gases you individually produce and has units of tonnes (or kg) of carbon dioxide equivalent. It is comprised of two elements:

▶ **PRIMARY FOOTPRINT** This roughly calculates how much CO_2 we are responsible for creating and emitting through burning fossil fuels for electricity, heating and transportation.

▶ **SECONDARY FOOTPRINT** This measures indirect CO_2 emissions created by the products that we use, the materials they are made from, and the processes that were used to create them.

Before you start to make changes to the green credentials of your property, it is a good idea to calculate your home's carbon footprint. There are many so-called 'Carbon Calculators' available:

▶ **THE GOVERNMENT** has developed the 'Act on CO_2' calculator (http://actonco2.direct.gov.uk) that will estimate your home's carbon footprint based on the age, type and size of your home, together with heating and electricity bills. The average UK household emits 6 tonnes of CO_2 per year. If you calculate your home's carbon footprint you can then look at ways of reducing it.

▶ **THE ENERGY SAVING TRUST** is an independent, non-profit making organisation that provides impartial information and advice specifically designed to help people take action to save energy and carbon. It has also created an excellent 'carbon cutter' calculator which offers just the advice we need (see page 187).

WHAT CHANGES CAN I MAKE?

To make things as clear as possible, I have broken down areas of green decision-making according to different aspects of domestic life. Within each area, there are key opportunities to make environmental improvements. You can decide whether to tackle the job yourself or whether to get a specialist to help. I've included a quick and easy guide to the costs and benefits of the job. You will then be able to decide which improvements are top priority for you.

The figures in this book are based on an average family energy spend – £1,000 per year split 50/50 between gas and electricity. The savings figures are based on the percentage savings that manufacturers suggest the green alternatives will create. Of course your home will be different – and if the price of energy fluctuates then the savings could increase or decrease. In some cases the percentage savings of green changes is not yet known and we are working with estimates that vary.

" **Reducing the temperature in your home by 1°C could cut your heating bill by 10%.** "

Green Home Improvements

WHY GO GREEN?

Many of the raw materials that we use when carrying out home improvements, such as stone or certain types of wood, are finite resources or are difficult to replace. Stone, which is taken from the ground and used in building work, is a non-renewable resource – we cannot produce more of it. Hardwoods, such as teak and mahogany, which grow in tropical areas, are slow-growing and stocks take a long time to be replaced, even if they are replanted. Equally, the production of certain materials – Portland cement, for example – can cause significant environmental damage. So, when making changes to our homes, it is a good idea to consider looking for greener alternatives to many of the conventional materials we are familiar with.

BEFORE YOU BEGIN

☑ **THINK OF THE BASICS**

Whenever you start to plan a job make sure that you know exactly how many materials you will need to use, whether it is paint, wood or plaster. Avoid buying too much of anything, because it runs the risk of simply being wasted. It will also save you time and money.

☑ **WEIGH UP THE PROS AND CONS OF ANY TASK**

The cost of 'going green' is sometimes dismissed as being too expensive, and in some cases it is true that 'green' materials are more costly than conventional products. But always consider – could this work pay off in the long term? Cheaper UPVC is often chosen instead of wooden windows, but it has a far shorter life span and pollution is caused by its production and disposal.

☑ **UNDERSTAND HOW TO USE YOUR ECO-FRIENDLY MATERIAL**

If you are using a contractor, it is worth choosing one who is familiar with, and has an interest in, 'green' materials.

☑ **BEFORE BUYING ALWAYS CONSIDER YOUR ALTERNATIVES**

Reduce, reuse, and recycle. Sometimes you may find something you already own that could substitute perfectly for a material you might otherwise have to buy. Be imaginative. Be creative.

☑ **CONDUCT YOUR RESEARCH THOROUGHLY**

This chapter offers ideas and guidance, but it is you who will have to choose products that fit your needs, and place your trust in companies who claim to be eco-friendly.

USING MATERIALS RESPONSIBLY

Always be careful when measuring up or deciding on how much material you need, whether it's fabric for curtains or gravel for the garden. Be as accurate as possible, and avoid any waste.

Re-use, renovate or restore materials you already have. This is one of the best ways of making 'green' improvements

Choose natural materials in preference to petroleum/ plastic-based products.

Choose materials that will be easily recyclable or biodegradable when they reach the end of their lives.

If you buy local materials, it will certainly reduce the distance they need to travel. However, materials from other parts of the country and certain imported goods are eco-friendly too – do your research.

BASIC BUILDING MATERIALS

Once you have decided to embark on a home improvement project you need to decide what materials you are going to use. Many conventional materials may be cheap and easily available but they are not always cheap for the environment. This section looks at different types of building and DIY materials, identifies the ones that are thought to cause more harm to the environment and why, and suggests some greener alternatives. These are becoming increasingly easy to source, either via the internet or even at your local DIY store, so shop around.

OVERVIEW OF BASIC BUILDING MATERIALS

WOOD AND TIMBER

The plight of forests and rainforests worldwide is well documented. It is estimated that they have reduced by half of their original extent and that we are still losing forests at an alarming rate, due to roads, development, logging and farming. Avoid using hardwoods such as teak from tropical rainforests. Sustainable, forested wood is a better option and is generally labelled as such (see pages 20–1).

BRICK

Bricks are made from clay in the ground and fired in a kiln. If we can reduce the amount of new bricks we buy, we reduce the need for quarrying, which in turn means kilns burning less energy and releasing less carbon into the atmosphere, which can only be a good thing.

CEMENT

Portland cement is used in building throughout the world. However, the manufacturing process does considerable damage to the atmosphere. Alternative mortars are available.

PLASTER

Plaster is a smooth mortar, usually used for finishing walls and ceilings and giving a smooth surface on which to apply paint or wallpaper. Plasters are now generally made from a variety of materials including gypsum or lime. The green credentials of each of these materials varies.

PAINT

Some paints are made using crude oil; a resource that we know only too well is running out fast. The production process used to make paint creates a huge amount of waste, and the paints themselves often include a number of ingredients that produce unpleasant fumes. Fortunately, there are now safer, healthier paints, containing fewer chemicals, which are well worth investigating.

GLUES, VARNISHES AND SEALANTS

Animal derivatives found in such products, produce hazardous air pollutants and the fumes contain volatile organic compounds (VOCs). Eco-adhesives are safer for you, your children and your pets. Glue is useful for all small household fixes – it is worth finding an eco-glue so that you can mend items rather than buying new.

TILING

Whether tiling is ceramic, terracotta, flagstone or limestone, stone itself is a non-renewable resource and supplies are finite. Any recycling and reclaiming is valuable. Not only does this help prolong the useful life of materials and help limit amounts of rubble in landfill sites, it saves the energy needed to produce new tiling from scratch.

🌳 WOOD & TIMBER

Wood has been used as a material since time began. It is a warm material that, with clever craftsmanship, can be manipulated to add grace to any home – and, properly maintained, it lasts indefinitely. However, the popularity of wood, is not without its consequences: a large percentage of the world's forests have been destroyed and it is important to be aware of the source of the timber we use. Whilst we can plant more trees, some grow quicker than others and their frequent felling affects the environment more or less. Buying timber can seem like a bit of an eco-minefield; fortunately, there are some relatively straightforward guidelines.

CHOOSING MATERIALS

☑ When buying wood you should consider the species: some types of wood take significantly longer to grow than others. Those that take the longest to grow are hardwoods that come from tropical and sub-tropical areas, such as teak and ebony. From a green perspective, they should be avoided as the rainforests where they grow are already under considerable threat and any commercial demand for hardwood will only place the remaining forests in greater danger. Sustainably produced woods from native European species, such as oak, beech, birch and pine, are increasingly available and certified sources mean that the forests are managed responsibly.

☑ Check for the Forest Stewardship Council (FSC) or Programme for the Endorsement of Forest Certification (PEFC) logo on any wood products you intend to purchase. These are international, independent, not-for-profit organisations which were established to promote the responsible management of the world's forests.

✔ Reclaimed timber is an environmental winner. There are many companies who specialise in salvaging all kinds of old wood and either recycle it into beautiful new products or sell it for your own use. These companies are often excellent sources of unusual furniture as well, so it is well worth hunting around before making a purchase.

✔ Recycled wood is often used for chipboard and MDF, as well as for wood chippings used in playgrounds or animal bedding. MDF is made from recovered wood fibres, consequently it reduces wood waste. It is compressed with adhesive into a smooth, strong surface, and it is very inexpensive compared to wood. However, it sometimes includes formaldehyde, an industrial fungicide, that can be toxic when inhaled. If possible, specify formaldehyde-free MDF.

GREEN ALTERNATIVE: BAMBOO

This favourite food of the panda is a great alternative to wood due to its strength, flexibility and sustainability. Bamboo can be harvested and replenished with considerably less impact to the environment. It can be selectively harvested annually, and is capable of regeneration without needing to be replanted. On the down side, bamboo can be an aggressive invader of nearby forests if not managed properly, and newly planted areas can lead to problems with erosion and to unsustainable farming practices. As with wood, it makes sense to check the source of any bamboo product.

FOREST STEWARDSHIP COUNCIL

The Forest Stewardship Council (FSC) – and also the Programme for the Endorsement of Forest Certification (PEFC) – provide standard setting, trademark assurance and accreditation services for companies and organisations interested in responsible forestry.

Products carrying the FSC label are independently certified to assure consumers that they come from forests that are managed to meet the social, economic and ecological needs of present and future generations. Forests provide us with clean water, fresh air and they even help combat global warming. They also provide food, medicine and important natural resources, such as timber and paper. If managed responsibly, forests and plantations benefit forest people and the global community. However, in some countries, as much as 80% of the timber is harvested illegally. This often involves violation of human rights and destruction of protected forests.

FSC certification offers forest managers rewards for managing their forests the FSC way – following the highest social and environmental criteria. In some instances rewards can be in the form of price premiums. But increasingly, FSC certification is rewarded with improved access to environmentally sensitive markets. Also, more and more governments and leading businesses are starting to specify FSC certified materials in their purchasing programmes.

Most large retailers will only supply FSC-certified timber as they want and need to be seen making greener choices. Online and smaller retailers (where public relations are of less importance) may supply non-sustainable wood. Be aware that it is sometimes hard to trace the chain of custody.

 The overall cost of FSC timber for DIY is often higher than non-FSC timber. However, in some cases FSC materials can be cheaper, and prices are likely to fall further in future as more producers become FSC-certified.

COMMITMENT TO RESPONSIBLE FORESTRY

FSC prohibits destruction of natural forests or other habitats around the world

FSC prohibits the use of highly hazardous pesticides around the world

FSC prohibits the cultivation of genetically modified trees (GMOs)

FSC respects the right of indigenous peoples around the world

FSC inspects each certified operation at least once a year – and if they are found not to comply, the certificate is withdrawn

 # BRICK

Many different varieties of brick have been used for construction in this country over the years; some are specific to local areas, and some are available nationwide. When starting a job that requires brickwork of any kind, whether it's a large extension or a wall in the garden, try to make an informed decision about the type of bricks you need. It is worth considering the use of reclaimed bricks, particularly if you already live in an older period property.

THE NEED FOR ALTERNATIVES

Bricks are made from clay that is taken from the ground and fired in a kiln to make it go hard. The production of new bricks requires a great deal of energy, both in terms of quarrying and the power used in firing. There is also the cost of transportation to stockists and then to consumers, to be taken in to consideration. Consequently, it is a good idea to look at alternatives.

RECLAIMED BRICKS

Old bricks from demolition sites cannot always be salvaged and are often rendered unusable, partly because the Portland cement used to lay the bricks has very strong bonding qualities and is very hard to clean off. However, for many years building rubble has been crushed and reused as hardcore (sometimes mixed with asphalt and concrete). The brick recycling industry is looking at other ways of using brick rubble. In a perfect world buildings would be carefully taken apart and all components reused. However, bricks are very difficult to clean, making this nearly impossible in some cases, and the time involved can make it non-cost effective. But there are now several companies who supply a wide variety of reclaimed bricks, with most offering matching services to help you find the very best brick for your job.

The price of bricks varies according to quality and style.

TYPE OF BRICK	NEW COST PER 100	RECLAIMED COST PER 100
Stock	£25–35	£60–100
Handmade	£50–80	£70–100
Wire cut	£15–25	£50–70

BRICK ALTERNATIVES

WOOD Buildings constructed from wood are part of Britain's heritage. Oak is particularly long lasting – there are oak-framed buildings dating from the 15th and 16th centuries. In recent years, the UK has been less keen to use timber for construction, while other countries (Scandinavia and the USA, for example), have been taking advantage of the high-energy efficiency and low environmental impact of wood for many years. However, today, there is much interest in eco-friendly timber-frame or log houses, whether they are of a traditional design or contemporary style.

As an alternative to using bricks, timber has many plus points including the fact that it usually costs less. It has a low embodied energy value (the amount of energy required by all of the activities associated with the production process) and it is an excellent insulator – a 2.5cm timber board has better thermal resistance than an 11.4cm brick wall. However, the issues of sustainability should be considered. If you are using new timber make sure that it comes from sustainable and legitimate sources. Also make sure that you use a bio-friendly timber preservative to extend its life.

STONE Stone is an alternative to brick but whether it is more environmentally friendly is arguable. Stone, like the clay for bricks, needs to be quarried, 'dressed' (cut and shaped) and transported, so there is an environmental impact. If you want to use stone rather than brick, check if it is possible to use locally quarried stone. It might even be possible in some areas to use stone from your own site (house or garden), which can offset some of this impact.

EARTH BLOCKS There are cutting-edge new ideas for brickwork and wall construction. It is possible to abandon brickwork altogether and consider earth blocks. These are construction blocks, which can be made of compressed chalk or earth (waste products), or from clay, sand and a stabilizing ingredient such as lime. The earth mixture is put into a press machine where it is compressed – the blocks are uniform in size and shape. Whether constructed from waste or new products, the blocks do not need to be fired in a kiln. They are laid in exactly the same way as a 'normal' brick.

COB BUILDING This traditional method, from Cumbria and southwest England, involves making buildings from dirt or mud. It has been around for centuries, dying out in the early 19th century, until a relatively recent interest in sustainable housing sparked a revival. Modern cob techniques remain much the same as traditional methods. It sounds simple, just mix soil, clay, sand and straw to a consistency like dough, and start your wall, but it's very labour intensive.

STRAW BALES The use of tightly bound straw bales as an alternative to bricks for construction has advantages for people and the planet; costs are low and so is the environmental impact. Straw probably has the lowest embodied energy of any building material. It is available in almost every area, consequently transportation costs are reduced and it is cheap to buy. It is also a sustainable resource with a short growth/harvest cycle; the UK alone produces tons of surplus straw every year.

Although this type of construction is generally chosen by committed green aficionados, houses built of straw bales, contrary to popular belief, are not flimsy and vulnerable, not a fire risk, nor are they at risk from pests, or only short term (some straw-bale homes in Nebraska USA are more than 100 years old). Straw bales also offer fantastic insulation, saving up to three-quarters of a home's heating costs. In addition, it seems that straw bales are easy to build with. They are stacked like huge bricks and walls can be erected quickly without much building experience. If this agricultural by-product became a mainstream building material, energy expenditures, the amount of straw burned, and the use of fossil fuels needed to transport materials would all be reduced.

Getting planning permission depends on the local authority and where you want to build. There is nothing specific to straw-bale construction in the building regulations, but they certainly conform to criteria concerning health and safety, fire resistance and energy efficiency. Problems may arise with neighbours or planning officials who are averse to anything new in their area. On the plus side, your ideas may fit in with local improvement plans, especially those regarding insulation levels and the use of natural materials.

DEALING WITH RUBBISH

Huge amounts of waste are generated, by individuals, households, businesses, construction and manufacturing industries. The disposal of this waste is an incredible burden, both to the economy and to the environment, and it is becoming increasingly important to focus on the amount of rubbish we are generating and what we do with it.

DIY BUILDING WASTE

A huge amount of waste is created by DIY jobs and it can be difficult to dispose of it properly. Only small quantities of DIY waste such as soil, brick, rubble, doors and windows will be accepted by your local authority so it may be advisable to hire a skip. Think carefully about whether you need to throw away a broken appliance or if it can be repaired. Try to be creative with your waste – broken tiles are useful for lining the bottom of a plant pot and unwanted paint can be given away to someone who needs it. Remember that the less you throw away; the smaller the impact on the environment.

Commercial and industrial waste includes waste generated by a builder, gardener, glazier or other tradesman working in a domestic property. It is carefully controlled by laws which determine where, how much and what type of waste can be disposed of. If you are paying someone to do the work the cost of waste removal should be included in your quote.

In the UK the predominant method of waste disposal has been to bury or 'landfill' much of its waste in the ground. The mining industry has left a network of large holes that can be used. These are lined to prevent gases escaping or contaminated liquids leaking into rivers and water supplies. Newer sites have systems to remove these pollutants altogether.

HOUSEHOLD WASTE RECYCLING CENTRES

Most local authorities in the UK run Household Waste Recycling Centres (HWRC) where homeowners (not commercial users) can recycle and dispose of their household waste. If you have undertaken a DIY project in your home own (and have not employed anyone to do the work) then you can often take the waste to the HWRC. Unusually frequent visits or high volumes of waste may require a permit or attract a charge and limits are usually applied to certain items, for example, 1 standard door, 100 litres of soil or 2 sacks of tiles. Make sure you look into what you can take before turning up at your local centre with a car full of rubbish.

RECYCLING

Government targets have been set to recycle or compost 33 per cent of household waste by 2015. Many countries, particularly in Europe, are years ahead of the UK in terms of what and how they recycle.

- **KERBSIDE SCHEMES** A kerbside recycling scheme is available to a majority of households in the UK. Many are restricted to paper, glass and cans, but others include plastic and garden waste.

- **RECYCLING CENTRES** Recycling centres accept a wide range of items including scrap metal, electrical goods, garden waste, books and clothing, paper, cans and glass.

- **COMPOSTING** It is important to keep organic matter out of waste intended for landfill to help reduce methane emissions. There are composting schemes available for houses without a garden.

- **FREECYCLE SCHEMES** Internet-based schemes exist to help you advertise items you want to give away free and enable you to make contact with people who want them.

⏻ CEMENT

The fine grey powder that we refer to as cement is made of a mixture of raw minerals (limestone or chalk and clay/sand/shale). It contributes to the production of mortar (for rendering or laying bricks) and, most importantly, concrete. Cement is the essential ingredient in concrete, which is now used in almost all building processes worldwide: the level of its consumption is second only to water. However, there is widespread debate about Portland cement and concrete as a green building material.

Portland cement is the main type of cement used in buildings throughout the world. It was invented in 1824 by a British bricklayer called Joseph Aspdin. Its name is derived from its similarity in colour to a type of stone quarried on the Isle of Portland in Dorset and is used to describe the process of manufacture (for instance, you can buy Blue Circle brand Portland cement). It eventually usurped lime mortar still found in many old buildings.

Cement is manufactured by combining the raw materials at a very high temperature in a kiln. The raw materials fuse together to form 'clinker', a hard granular substance The clinker is ground to a powder along with gypsum to make cement. Cement manufacturers face a number of challenges on green issues: they use reserves of raw materials, burn fossil fuels (in the kilns) and in so doing create carbon dioxide emissions to the atmosphere. But, at the same time, cement makes a huge contribution to sustaining our quality of life with regard to our homes (other buildings, roads, reservoirs etc). While manufacturers are under pressure to reduce emissions and make the process cleaner, it is a race against time with demand increasing and nobody wanting prices to rise.

NEW PRODUCTS

New technology has allowed alternatives to emerge. These are not yet available to the domestic market but will become more widespread in the future. The down side is that most cost more.

▶ **GGBS (GROUND GRANULATED BLASTFURNACE SLAG)** Also known as slag cement, GGBS involves no quarrying, less energy and is made from blastfurnace slag, which is a by-product of the steel industry.

▶ **AIRCRETE** More expensive than cement, this foam-based product requires less energy to produce, and is both light and strong. Excellent for insulation and usually used to construct blocks for new buildings.

▶ **CERAMICRETE** A phosphate ceramic that produces a substance even stronger than concrete. An additional bonus is that industrial waste can be used within its manufacture.

▶ **C-FIX** A relatively new kind of cement, also known as carbon concrete, a thermoplastic heavy-duty binder developed by Shell and the University of Delft. It is made using waste from oil refineries.

RESPONSIBLE CEMENT PRODUCTION

Cement manufacturers are trying to stop pollution, which includes dust, gases, noise and vibration when operating machinery and during blasting in quarries. Equipment to reduce dust emissions during quarrying for raw materials and manufacture of cement is widely used, and use of equipment to trap and separate exhaust gases is also increasing. Environmental protection also includes the re-integration of disused quarries by returning them to nature or landscaping them. In addition the cement industry uses over 1.1 million tonnes of waste as an alternative fuel or raw material that would otherwise have gone into landfill sites or incineration.

CHOOSING MATERIALS

Portland cement became popular because it could be produced quickly and it dries fast, and in the second half of the 20th century demand for rapid building was high. Consequently, traditional lime cement was almost forgotten. However, many would agree that traditional buildings constructed of stone and brick benefit, both physically and aesthetically, from lime mortars, renders and plasters.

LIME MORTAR

A traditional building material, lime has fantastic green credentials:

➡ It needs less energy to produce than cement.

➡ When it dries it re-absorbs carbon dioxide gases and because it dries slowly, it gains strength over a longer period of time than its quick-drying counterpart.

➡ It is flexible and, therefore, less damaging to brickwork.

➡ Unlike Portland cement, it allows bricks and stone to be recycled easily after demolition – cement mortar is often harder than old brick.

➡ It is resilient, durable and water resistant. Because it breathes, it is ideal for use in modern green 'earth' structures, such as earth blocks or even cob buildings.

1 kg of wet mortar per brick is about the average amount needed. 50 kg of ready-mixed mortar will produce around 60kg of wet mortar.

LABOUR

Tradesmen skilled in using lime products may charge more than those who are used to working with conventional materials because it is a skill that is less commonly required.

PRODUCT	COST
Lime mortar	25 kg bags are available for approximately £10
Ready-mixed mortar	20 kg bags are available for approximately £4

" The cement industry is playing an important role in minimising some of the UK's waste disposal problems by processing selected wastes and by-products from other industries into alternative raw materials or fuels for use in the cement kiln. "

PLASTER

Plaster has been used to line interior walls and ceilings for centuries. Traditionally a mix of lime, sand and horsehair or straw was used for the first coat or 'render', with lime and water as a second 'set' coat. Lime is still used today for its breathable and flexible qualities, but much more rarely. Most plaster used internally is gypsum-based with different additives. The use of raw materials and cement in the manufacture of plaster means it creates similar environmental problems to that of cement.

CHOOSING MATERIALS

Although they can be expensive, natural clays, recycled and reclaimed aggregates and hemp are used to create a smooth wall. You can buy plaster that uses natural ingredients such as plant extracts, chalk and quartz, although lime is the most commonly used. They help buildings to breathe more easily and are available in a variety of textures.

USING ECO-PLASTERS

You will need to assess your building and decide which is the most appropriate material to use. If the original stone or brick is soft, then the plaster should ideally be even softer. Ideally, you should repair using something similar to the existing or original material.

Lime-based mortars, renders, plasters and limewashes work well, but are more difficult to use. Check that your contractor knows how to apply the materials as they are often blamed for poor results.

Natural interior plasters are available in 6 kg packs for between £25 and £35 depending on your needs. Lime plasters are available in tubs of 25 kg for around £7.

 # PAINT

Volatile organic compounds (VOCs) are added to paints to slow down the drying process, which helps to get a smoother finish. They also make products last longer, work better and make them easier to use. However, there are increasing concerns about the impact of the chemicals used in most paints on our health and the environment. Using paints that have a low level of VOCs can help not only your health but also the environment.

CHOOSING ECO-FRIENDLY PAINT

VOCs are carbon-based chemical compounds that evaporate easily in the atmosphere, and are known to be a contributor to global climate change. Many of them are also linked with numerous health problems (such as asthma, headaches and skin disorders). Consequently, there is a growing market in low- or no-VOC paints. Since 2004 conventional paint companies have been forced by EU environmental regulations to significantly reduce their VOC content, and many large paint companies now offer at least one variety of non-toxic paint. However, many of these still contain VOC solvents, chemical pigments and fungicides. Here are some tips on what to look out for when choosing paint.

➡ Brands that show labels with a full ingredient list are particularly helpful. Some paints may be branded 'organic' but may still contain petrochemicals. Always check the ingredients and the list is missing, it is better to look elsewhere for your paint.

➥ Many brands of paint show the percentage of Volatile Organic Compounds (VOCs) in their product. Millions of tonnes of VOCs from paints are released into the atmosphere each year: by choosing paint with low VOCs your health and your family's will benefit and you'll be doing your bit for the environment.

➥ Be aware that some 'natural' products may come from GM plantations or unethical sources. Check the manufacturers' websites if you want further details.

➥ Try to avoid solvent-based paint, white spirit, turpentine or similar harmful chemicals and heavy metals such as cadmium. Use water-based paint as an eco-friendly alternative.

➥ 'Greener' paints are often called Low-VOC, No-VOC, VOC-Free, odourless, odour-free and green, natural or organic paints. Be aware that there are no set standards for defining these labels, and they can be misused for marketing purposes.

➥ DIY supplier B&Q have initiated a VOC labelling system used to show that the paint has fulfilled certain environmental requirements, and to indicate the content of VOCs using one of five classifications: Minimal (0-0.29%), Low, Medium, High and Very High (VOC content greater than 50%).

➥ Paints containing petrochemicals can release harmful gases (see page 39). Natural paints can ease symptoms for allergy sufferers and help regulate humidity in a room, due to their 'breathability'.

➥ Different eco-friendly brands will offer a variety of advantages and corresponding drawbacks. One paint may be marginally less eco-friendly than another, but could give you a better result. It is a balancing act so do as much research as you can.

WHAT IS WRONG WITH OLDER PAINTS?

- Production of more traditional paints can produce at least as much again in solid waste and sometimes a lot more.

- Both 'standard' paints and some natural paints can contain solvents, which are made using crude oil. Petrochemicals are used in the production of synthetic solvents, resulting in dangerous and non-degradable waste.

- Synthetic paints can be more susceptible to fire, and the fumes are particularly harmful to people and the environment.

- Binders are part of the three main components of 'standard' paint, along with solvents and pigment. Plastic-based binders can actually attract dust as they become statically charged, creating more dust in the home and discomfort for allergy sufferers.

 This varies considerably according to the choice of paint and the size of the job. Here is a cost comparison guide.

PAINT TYPE	COST
Eco-paint	46–87p per sq. m
Leading brand	37–43p per sq. m
Store brand	37p per sq. m

RECYCLING

PAINT
You can dispose of leftover paint via your local household waste disposal centre, or if you have a reasonable amount, you can give it away to someone who needs it via your local Freecycle website (see page 188).

EMPTY POTS
Unfortunately, not all recycling centres will accept empty paint cans. Check with your local council.

ECO-FRIENDLY PAINTS: COMMON CONCERNS

CHOICE
It is certainly true that eco-friendly brands offer a more limited range of colours but there are still plenty to choose from.

QUALITY
Organic and water-soluble paints have been known to wash or rub off easily and can require up to five coats. However, many brands have now overcome these difficulties.

DRYING
Many eco-friendly paints do take longer to dry than conventional paints.

GLUES & SEALANTS

Many of us assume that effective glues have to be chemical-based. However, the Romans used pine-wood tar and beeswax as a waterproof glue for shipbuilding, and beeswax is still used today as a reliable adhesive, so there are viable alternatives. For instance, water-based adhesives are a popular alternative to solvent-based adhesives because of their lower VOC levels and tendency to be non-toxic and environmentally friendly.

Most glues and sealants are toxic because of the VOC levels present. There are many different products on the market, some containing resins, formaldehydes, and silicones – all varying in degrees of toxicity. The packaging will include details of all the hazardous ingredients.

INGREDIENTS TO AVOID

- Solvents and white spirit
- Animal products
- Heavy metals eg. lead, mercury
- Formaldehyde
- VOCs
- Chlorine

GREEN ALTERNATIVES

- Water-based products
- Natural binders
- Natural pigments, e.g. titanium oxide, yellow ochre
- Mineral fillers, e.g. clay, limestone
- Natural thickeners, e.g. resin
- Natural waxes

There are key criteria for defining a glue or sealant as eco-friendly. Its formula should be free from ingredients such as hazardous air pollutants and ozone depletors. Glues and sealants can also be green because they reduce the environmental impact of a building (e.g., the energy efficiency gained from the effective use of sealants). Finally, there are products that contribute to a safe and healthy indoor environment (e.g., low VOCs or formaldehyde-free adhesives).

WHERE CAN I FIND ECO-FRIENDLY PRODUCTS?

There are many organisations that can help you make green choices, with information on where to buy eco-materials, such as Friends of the Earth (see page 186).

TIPS FOR AVOIDING TOXIC CHEMICALS IN YOUR HOME

We can't and don't need to avoid all chemicals: some are natural and occur in our food, featuring in most of our working lives. What we can try to avoid are some man-made chemicals in the home as they are strongly suspected, and sometimes proven, to be linked to health problems.

➡ 'Green-friendly' – don't always believe the label. Lots of companies claim 'eco' and 'green' credentials, but do read the actual ingredients on the label and avoid those with more suspect chemicals (see opposite).

➡ Look for products that are chlorine-free – chlorine bleach is toxic to aquatic life and so damaging as it works it way out through drains. It's not great for humans, either.

➡ Make sure the label says 'Low VOC' which means there are fewer petrochemicals that give out harmful volatile organic compounds (VOCs), which trigger asthma and other respiratory problems.

RISKS ASSOCIATED WITH TOXIC CHEMICALS

The risk from toxic chemicals comes from the fact that the effects of inhaling them are so unpredictable. You might breathe in a certain amount and appear okay, and then could inhale the same amount on another occasion and become sick. It takes the body at least two weeks to rid itself of these toxic chemicals through the urine and through exhaling, which is why the breath of someone using chemicals often has a chemical smell.

There are thousands of different chemicals classified as volatile organic compounds. A few of the less safe and commonly found VOCs are:

CHEMICAL NAME	HOW IT AFFECTS THE BODY
Formaldehyde	thought to be carcinogenic
Benzene	thought to be carcinogenic
Toluene	linked to neurological damage
Xylene	linked to neurological damage
Perchloroethylene	thought to be the cause of central nervous system damage

Because VOCs are unstable, they can be released from the walls into the air as the paint or glue is applied or as it dries, and even once dry. This, combined with the fact that paint, for instance, is usually applied to a large area, can cause people living or spending time in these freshly painted homes to have exposures to VOCs that are much greater than normal – as much as 1,000 times greater. This can cause headaches and other potential health problems such as asthma.

Although there is a lack of data about acceptable levels of specific chemicals, it makes sense to use low VOC products and to work in well-ventilated rooms if you are using solvents and paints. Not a lot is known about indoor air pollution, so it is a good idea to take these simple precautions.

The definition of a VOC is based on evaporation into the atmosphere, rather than reactivity, and British coatings suppliers have adopted a labelling scheme for all decorative coatings to inform customers about the levels of organic solvents and other volatile materials present. Split into five levels, or 'bands', these span Minimal, Low, Medium, High, and Very High.

Not everyone is affected by VOCs, but it makes sense to avoid the harmful chemicals that are associated with health problems.

> **Adhesives** and sealants are an important part of the green building process in two areas: by improving a building's energy efficiency and by minimising the effects on the environment and air quality.

SOURCE QUOTE: ADHESIVE & SEALANT MAGAZINE

 FLOORING

When sourcing eco-friendly flooring there are various criteria to consider. Ideally you are looking for something made from renewable materials that have been sustainably harvested, without too much damage to the environment, which will stand the test of wear and tear and fashion time and will biodegrade after disposal. Ideally, look for a production process that does not use chemical treatments or toxic materials.

WOOL CARPET

Critics have recently been concerned by the environmental impact of sheep and, therefore, wool production. Though I believe the more natural the better. A truly luxurious option as well as a greener one, wool has many advantages over synthetic carpet. It is resilient, anti-static and biodegradable if it has a natural backing. However, wool carpet may not be suitable for bathrooms. Also it is more expensive than man-made carpet.

CORK

Derived from the bark of the cork oak tree, which can be stripped from the tree every ten years, cork flooring is naturally renewable. It is durable, soft underfoot and provides heat and sound insulation. It is also resistant to fire, rot, water and staining, making it suitable for use in all rooms in the house.

SUSTAINABLE WOOD

Most large UK suppliers source wood from properly managed forests. Wood will last indefinitely as long as it is well maintained – it must be sealed and treated to protect from water and other wear and tear.

NATURAL LINOLEUM

Distinct from its synthetic namesake, natural linoleum is made from linseed oil, pine resin and cork, which are all both natural and renewable. It is durable, comfortable to walk on, stain- and water-resistant and extremely versatile. Although it is low maintenance, the smell of linseed oil may be off-putting to some people and it is highly flammable.

BAMBOO

A real alternative to wood flooring in terms of strength, durability and colour range. Bamboo is also entirely sustainable, as it is a fast-growing grass with a short growing cycle before it reaches maturity. However it is not suitable for all rooms as it can warp when exposed to excessive moisture. Check that non-toxic adhesives have been used during production and installation.

COIR

Made from the fibre found on the husk of the coconut, coir has been used as a natural flooring material for hundreds of years. It has a unique rustic look, is extremely durable, can provide both heat and sound insulation and is 100% biodegradeable. On the down side it is rough and not comfortable for sitting on for long periods and it can be difficult to source.

JUTE

Jute is derived from the inner bark of a tropical herb called *Corchorus* that is grown in southern Asia. The fast-growing plants are a great renewable resource. Traditionally used to make sacks, jute has a variety of uses including cloth, soft furnishings and rope. It also makes flooring that is durable, fade-resistant, anti-static, fire-resistant. However, it breaks down when it gets wet and can be attacked by microbes.

# TILES

The chief green issue surrounding tile production is the quarrying of the materials used to make them, such as clay, slate, marble and limestone. Quarries create high levels of dust, waste and noise pollution. However, there are a number of alternatives worth investigating.

RECYCLED GLASS TILES

Recycled glass tiles are generally made from recycled glass bottles and are suitable for use in kitchens and bathrooms. As well as reducing the amount of glass that ends up in landfill, they even use less energy to manufacture than making glass tiles from scratch.

RECYCLED CERAMIC TILES

Recycled ceramic tiles, made from glass and a variety of waste products, are less common but offer durability as well as the attractive aesthetic quality of a traditional ceramic tile.

RECLAIMED TILES

Search for local companies that source reclaimed tiles including Victorian or terracotta tiles and you may unearth something remarkable. Prices of reclaimed tiles vary according to quality, scarcity, age and demand.

RECYCLED METAL TILES

These are constructed from recycled aluminium, a metal that can be recovered from all kinds of different areas. A clean and efficient and unusual flooring idea.

RUBBER TILES

Rubber tiles are extremely versatile and can be used on walls and floors in any room in the house. They are easy to clean, easy to fit, and available in a wide selection of colours. Rubber tiles are also durable, great at soundproofing and non-slip. Rubber in all its forms is regarded as an eco-friendly material, but, if you are looking for the lowest environmental impact, then choose natural virgin rubber sourced from trees, and harvested in a responsible manner. Avoid synthetic rubber, which is a by-product of crude oil. Recycled rubber is even better from an environmental and a financial point of view, as it is cheaper and more durable than new rubber.

> Using recycled materials in the manufacturing process uses considerably less energy than that required for producing new products from raw materials – even when comparing all associated costs including transport etc.

SOURCE QUOTE: RECYCLE NOW

WINDOWS AND DOORS

Windows and exterior doors suffer from wear and tear: they are used every day, and are exposed to the sun, rain and wind. Over time, if they are not properly maintained, paint can flake and rain will get to the wood, making it swell and rot, and metal-framed windows will rust. Without a doubt, the 'greenest' way to deal with the problem is to maintain and repair existing windows and doors so that they last. Replacement is costly, although arguably, can end up being eco-friendly. For instance, double glazing can result in savings in energy consumption, which benefits the environment.

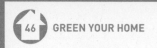 WINDOWS

If you are considering making energy-efficient improvements, windows are a critical area to target, particularly if you are renovating a run-down property and the windows need more than just painting. A huge amount of heat escapes from small gaps in windows, and thin, single-glazed windows allow much of the heat generated inside to escape Whether you decide to renovate or replace, make sure improvements to windows are green ones – it's an area well worth investigating.

RENOVATING WINDOWS

If you live in an older property, consider all the options (environmental, aesthetic and financial) before replacing windows. Whatever type of windows you have – usually casement or sash – they can very often be repaired. If they are wooden, only part of a frame may need to be replaced not the whole thing.

In terms of energy efficiency, windows need to be draught-proof, ideally with double glazing. Window renovation specialists offer a service to remove sash units from the frame so that they can be properly repaired and restored. They can also upgrade the window's performance by installing a sealing system to improve energy efficiency without altering the appearance of the window. This costs £300–500 for a standard 1 x 1.5m window depending on the condition of the glazing and frame and the level of repair.

Most double-glazed windows now come as sealed units, complete with frame and glass, instead of each pane of glass being individually double glazed. The two layers of glass have a gas between them and are sealed around the edges, giving maximum insulation effectiveness. However, it is possible to get frameless double-glazed units to repair existing windows but, clearly, these have to be made to measure.

BUYING NEW WINDOWS

If you live in a conservation area or in a listed building, you will need to check with your Local Authority as to what you can and can't do. The general rule is that you replace like with like – for instance, if you need to replace sash windows in Victorian or Georgian properties, they should be replaced with copies (made from sustainable wood) that look the same as the originals.

However, building regulations require any replacement window MUST be double-glazed. Modern glass can have insulating properties that help keep you cool in the summer and warm in the winter. But before you replace any windows you will need to consider a few key points:

- **STRUCTURAL ISSUES** If you are planning to fit windows of a different shape to your existing ones, you will probably need planning permission and building regulations approval for any structural changes.

- **DESIGN** The style of your existing windows may not provide adequate natural lighting to the living space. A different design could dramatically improve things to make sure the windows do not fight the architectural style of the building itself.

- **DAMP** Wooden windows tend to rot due to poor maintenance, allowing moisture into the woodwork. Make sure you rectify any damp issues.

MATERIALS

The question of the materials used to make new window frames arouses strong feelings.

▶ **UPVC** (uplasticised polyvinyl chloride) windows certainly provide appropriate levels of energy efficiency but their production creates toxins that pollute the atmosphere. They are low maintenance while they last but do need to be replaced after about 25 years.

▶ **TIMBER** is a natural, environmentally friendly material, provided it is responsibily sourced. Timber windows do need regular maintenance every 3–5 years but they will last indefinately.

REGULATIONS

Since 1 April 2002, all new or replacement windows have had to meet the thermal insulation requirements of building regulations to prevent unnecessary energy loss. Windows must achieve a certain U-value – the lower the U-value, the lower the heat loss. If you are changing windows, this will almost certainly mean transferring from single-glazed windows to double-glazed windows. Additional insulation can be gained by using low-emissivity coated glass, or filling the gap in double-glazing with an inert gas such as argon or xenon.

WINDOW ENERGY RATING

The British Fenestration Rating Council (BFRC) is an independent, government-backed initiative established to enhance the energy efficiency of buildings. BFRC in conjunction with the UK glazing industry and European partners has developed a Window Energy Rating to assess the energy performance of domestic windows. For domestic customers the rating value is given on a scale of A–G. In April 2006 the BFRC Rating for windows was included as part of building regulations. The standard for replacement windows in an existing dwelling should be an energy rating of 'E' or better and the standard for new windows in extensions should be a 'D' Rating or better.

ENERGY EFFICIENT WINDOW RATINGS LABEL

Each window rated by the BFRC has a unique label, which displays the overall rating level (A, B, C etc, where A is the most efficient rating), the energy index rating, the climate zone, the window U value, the solar heat gain and the effective heat loss due to air penetration (L). This determines how well a window will be able to conserve heat, keep the wind out, resist condensation and improve sound insulation.

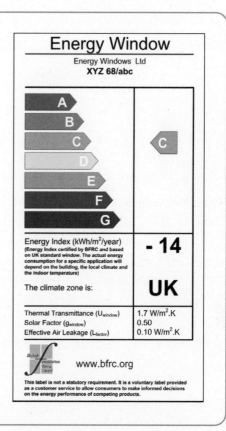

Energy Window

Energy Windows Ltd
XYZ 68/abc

A
B
C
D
E
F
G

C

Energy Index (kWh/m²/year)
(Energy Index certified by BFRC and based on UK standard window. The actual energy consumption for a specific application will depend on the building, the local climate and the indoor temperature)

- 14

The climate zone is:

UK

Thermal Transmittance (U$_{window}$)   1.7 W/m².K
Solar Factor (g$_{window}$)   0.50
Effective Air Leakage (L$_{factor}$)   0.10 W/m².K

www.bfrc.org

This label is not a statutory requirement. It is a voluntary label provided as a customer service to allow consumers to make informed decisions on the energy performance of competing products.

DOORS

Although doors have less impact than windows on the average home's energy bills, their performance is still extremely environmentally relevant. Older doors, particularly exterior doors, are often very draughty, and if this is the case, fitting draught excluders or even replacing them might be a good investment.

TYPES OF DOORS

INTERIOR WOODEN DOORS When purchasing wooden doors, do not forget that certain woods are harvested in an unsustainable way. To avoid this, choose doors made from FSC-certified wood. Although building regulations do not yet require it, ensure that your internal doors are well insulated to keep the heat where you want it.

GARAGE DOORS will affect the temperature of your garage or even your home if your garage is an integral part of the house.

PATIO DOORS are often energy-inefficient, but there are some improved options on the market such as:

- Thermal break systems, which trap air between two parts, offering superior insulation.

- Low-E (low emissivity) glass where a special metal coating controls the flow of rays in and out of your windows keeping rooms warm in winter and cool in summer.

TYPE OF DOOR	COST
Interior wood door	£60–120
Garage door depending on material	£300–500
Patio doors	£1,300–2,500
Glass doors (French doors)	£1,500–3,000
Single glass door	£450
Metal frame door	£159
Hardwood frame door	£49

PREVENTING HEAT LOSS

Heat may be lost through the door core and frame, through leaks around the door, and through glass – in the case of patio doors or doors with windows and glass elements. An energy-efficient door can dramatically reduce all these sources of heat loss. In some cases, storm doors, airlock vestibules, windbreaks and the location of the door (out of the path of prevailing winds) are also factors you should consider.

 GLASS

Make sure that the glass components of your doors are double or triple-paned, and that the glass is a low emissivity (low-E) type.

✔ FRAMES AND CORE MATERIALS

Door materials have a big impact on heat flow. Metal-clad doors tend to be more efficient than solid wooden doors. Highly efficient exterior doors are made of fibreglass, wood or steel (garage and entry doors) with polyurethane foam or other insulation layers included.

✔ WEATHERSTRIPPING (SEALING)

Energy-efficient doors are insulated and tightly sealed to prevent air from leaking through or around them. Make sure your doors are properly insulated and have door sweeps at the bottom to prevent draughts. Add draught-proofing tape (weatherstripping) around the frame. In some cases, insulated storm doors are also helpful, since they may provide an additional barrier to cold air. Consider this on internal as well as external doors.

> **If everyone in the UK draught proofed around doors and windows, we'd save nearly £200 million per year!**

SOURCE QUOTE: ENERGY SAVING TRUST

GREEN INSULATION

Like a warm winter coat, a cosy home needs to be well insulated. There are lots of ways of insulating your home – simple techniques such as tight-fitting windows and roof insulation, or major renovations such as double glazing. All insulation is green because it makes your home more energy-efficient. Without it up to one third of the heat you pay for – an average of £160 per year in a three-bed house – is lost through your roof, walls, windows and floors. Today's trend for open-plan living makes it tougher to heat homes efficiently and, in such homes, there's an even greater need for really effective insulation.

CHANGING TIMES

It is important to remember that we now live differently to how people did when many of our houses were built. Then people insulated themselves by wearing lots of clothes, in addition to direct heat from a range or open fire. Now we like to heat a whole house and so sealing up draughts is much more relevant. The downside is that old houses benefit from a certain amount of airflow so a balance is the best solution.

IS MY HOME SUITABLE?

The answer is yes, the majority of homes could have better insulation. It is not as visibly green as, say, installing solar panels but insulating your home is one of the easiest things you can do to reduce your carbon footprint, by keeping heat in during the winter. If you live in a contemporary open-plan house or an older property that has had small rooms made into one large living area, insulation is particularly crucial to help keep your home warm and comfortable. Even if you live in a flat you can reduce heat loss and cut your heating bills by following a few simple steps.

> " If everyone in the UK installed loft insulation, we could save £700 million and four million tonnes of CO_2 every year. "

SOURCE QUOTE: ENERGY SAVING TRUST

ARE GRANTS AVAILABLE?

Insulation suppliers are obliged to provide customers with advice on improving the energy efficiency of their homes. The value of grants can be up to £2,700 in total, but they vary within the UK. For example, in many areas grants are available for families, for the elderly or those on benefits. There are also initiatives where an assessor will visit your home and suggest improvements which could then be subsidised.

CHOOSING MATERIALS

All insulation makes a positive contribution to the environment by helping you to use less energy to keep your home warm. But bear in mind that not all insulators are 'green'. However, a growing range of eco-friendly options are available alongside traditional insulation materials, allowing us to save money on energy bills, without literally costing the earth.

- Look out for insulators that are made from organic materials such as wool or hemp – they are the most eco-friendly and score heavily over conventional or traditional materials because less energy was required to make them in the first place.

- Avoid products that will produce poisonous gases in a fire, and bear in mind the amount of energy it has taken to make the material and which chemicals were used in its production.

Insulating your home using green materials may not be the cheapest option but you may find it is worth making the extra green commitment when it is time to make your final decision.

INSULATING MATERIALS

After choosing the method of insulation that best suits your skills and space, you can then choose the material that suits your green budget. Insulation comes in several forms: rolls and batts (slabs), which are pre-cut sections of felt or fibre that make it simple to lay if the area you are insulating is easy to reach, such as an attic or loft; sheets, which come in boards that you will need to have cut to length and are used to insulate the sides of a roof; granules; and foam.

⇨ WOOL-BASED PRODUCTS

Wool-based products are made from a blend of wool from sheep with coarse fleeces unsuitable for clothing. It has many advantages and can be used for a variety of insulating tasks. It is breathable and can absorb moisture with no loss of thermal efficiency. For this reason it is effective at keeping buildings warm in winter. During warm conditions it releases moisture, which actually has a cooling effect. It is environmentally friendly: its production takes a fraction of the energy required to produce glass fibre insulation. It is completely safe to handle. It has an indefinite life expectancy and is easily recyclable.

⇨ HEMP-BASED PRODUCTS

Hemp-based products are a superb natural insulator, made from fibres from the hemp plant and recycled cotton fibres, held together using a thermoplastic binder. They are simple to install, non-irritant to touch. Fire and pest resistance is added through treatment with inorganic salts. Suitable for use as loft, wall and underfloor insulation, but should not be used as either cavity wall insulation or to insulate florring at ground level.

FLAX-BASED PRODUCTS

Flax-based products are made from the fibres of the flax plant, held together with natural binders. Like wool and hemp products it is ideal for floor and loft insulation, as well as the wall cavities of timber-framed construction. It has high thermal and sound insulation properties, it is safe to use and install.

ECO-FRIENDLY FIBREGLASS

Although you might not think that it is green, fibreglass manufacturers are incorporating recycled materials into their products and it is worth checking on the product details.

CELLULOSE PRODUCTS

Chemically treated for fire and mould resistance, cellulose insulation typically comprises 85% recycled content (such as recycled newsprint, jute sacking) with 15% fire-retardant and insect-resistant chemicals such as borax. It has insulation properties that are either equivalent to, or superior to, conventional loft insulation and is already widely used in the UK. Cellulose products also come in batt (slab) form.

ECO-FRIENDLY FOAM INSULATION

Low-density spray foam is quick to install, and it doesn't emit harmful gases. There are two green products: soy insulation, made up of soybean oil-based polyurethane, and water-based sprays with an insulation and air barrier. The one main advantage of foam is that it stops the air escaping by filling all the gaps. However, although it works in the short term it renders slates and tiles unable to be reused.

Other environmentally friendly loft insulation alternatives you may wish to explore include wood, fibreboard, cork and strawboard.

MATERIALS	COST
Wool-based products	£5-11 per sq. m depending on thickness (Thermafleece)
Hemp-based products	£5-11 per sq. m depending on thickness (Isovlas))
Flax-based products	£5-10 per sq. m depending on thickness (Isovlas)
Eco-friendly fibreglass	£3.30 per sq. m
Cellulose products	£3.60 per sq. m (Warmcel 00)
Eco-friendly foam insulation	About £6 per sq. m

INSULATION: POINTS TO REMEMBER

Renewable: is the product made from a renewable material ?

Local products: how far has the product travelled to reach your home?

Disposable: can the material be recycled?

Subsidies: can you get a government grant to cover the cost of your material?

Ease of use: is the product easy to install in your roof space?

Water resistance: in the event of a leak is the product able to dry out?

⊟ INSULATING WINDOWS

Ill-fitting or loose windows can allow draughts of cold air in and hot air out, and decrease your home's energy-efficiency. There are a number of ways you can address this issue. This section covers improving insulation for existing windows (see also Windows, pages 45–9).

As well as saving energy, insulating your windows brings other advantages, such as reduced noise from outside (and it also means you can make more noise yourself!) and less infiltration of dust and pollen.

SECONDARY GLAZING

▸ **TEMPORARY** A quick fix – ideal if you have just moved into a draughty flat in the winter. You can buy plastic film from most hardware shops and make your own.

▸ **PERMANENT** Secondary glazing with a frame to hold the glass/plastic that can be slid open or removed altogether for cleaning. Make sure that all window furniture (handles, hinges etc.) is tightly fitted and add draught excluders around the edges.

DOUBLE GLAZING

How does it work? Double glazing traps air or gas between two panes of glass, creating an insulating barrier that reduces heat loss, noise and condensation. Additionally, a low-emissivity coating on the inside

£	MATERIALS	COST
	Timber Sash Window	£665–1,060 per window including installation
	Metal Casement Window	£510–£675 per window

of the double glazed unit reduces the heat transference through the window. Usually, replacement, double-glazed windows come in sealed units that can be fitted into wood, metal or uPVC frames.

HOW LONG WILL THEY LAST?

Properly maintained, wooden frames last indefinitely. UPVC is generally guaranteed for 25 years. You may find that uPVC is a cheaper option but wood has better heat retention and noise reduction properties than uPVC; and it is better for the environment as uPVC is made using vinyl chloride which is thought to be harmful.

WILL I NEED PLANNING PERMISSION?

Planning permission is not normally required if the windows are the same size as those they are replacing. However, if the building is listed or is in a conservation area, you may well need listed building or conservation area consent. Always consult your Local Authority.

DO I NEED TO CONFORM TO BUILDING REGULATIONS?
All replacement windows in England and Wales are subject to building regulations. Again, contact your Local Authority for exact requirements.

IMPROVING EXISTING WINDOWS

There are some steps you can take to improve the efficiency of your existing windows. Options include: caulking, if you don't want them to open, or weatherstripping to reduce heat loss from draughty windows, and fitting shutters, blinds or, most effective, thick, interlined curtains to reduce heat loss.

SEALING WINDOWS

The best way to seal gaps in windows and doors is to apply an adhesive draught excluder. These are available on a roll and are stuck around the edge so that when the window or door is shut a firm seal is created reducing the draught. It is also possible to have a sealing system installed by a window specialist (see page 46).

SHUTTERS

Shutters control light, retain heat, add privacy when closed and provide full visibility when folded back. They can be fitted café style, tier-on-tier or full height. Wooden shutters can be either painted or stained. While there is a large discrepancy in the cost of shutters depending on the size and shape of window, they are a high-value item. Although expensive, shutters are extremely durable, have a long life expectancy and can provide additional security. If you're lucky enough to have original interior window shutters in your home, then it's advisable to retain them.

WOODEN BLINDS

If shutters are too expensive you could consider wooden Venetian blinds. Similar finishes to shutters are available, they are easy to measure and install, and are retractable for an unobstructed view. However, sufficient width may not be available for larger windows and they tend to be less durable than wooden shutters.

CURTAINS

Thick curtains can greatly reduce heat loss through windows. If the curtains are interlined they are even more effective. Ideally, they should fit closely to windows and should not cover radiators. In the evening, make sure that curtains (or blinds) are closed. The costs involved vary enormously, depending on whether you buy inexpensive ready-made curtains or have expensive made-to-measure curtains. The type and quality of the fabric used in either ready-made or made-to-measure will, of course, have an impact on cost.

TYPE	COST
Curtains	Ready-made curtains are available from £5, but can cost more than £2,000
Blinds	£5–70
Shutters	Vary in price according to style, but range from £150–300 per metre

ROOF & LOFT INSULATION

According to the Energy Saving Trust, if your loft is not insulated, 25% or over £100 per year of your heating bill is lost through your roof.

Before you start, check the thickness of your loft insulation between the joists. If you already have insulation it may be that it has been installed to the old standard, i.e., 50 mm or 100 mm thick. Experts tell us that we need to insulate to a depth of 270 mm to create savings, so existing insulation may need topping up.

Use caution when laying insulation over cables as they may overheat, or under the cold-water tank if it is at ceiling level, as it could freeze.

FLOOR INSULATION

Insulating certain floors is a job you can do yourself and it will help reduce heat loss and save you money on heating bills.

FLOORBOARDS

If you have floorboards, you can lift them and lay mineral wool insulation between the joists. Also you can use a sealant to fill gaps between floorboards and skirting boards to prevent draughts. Alternatively, if you have very old floorboards with wide gaps that you want to seal, you can hire a sanding machine that will polish the boards, and at the same time provide you with wood chips that you can put to one side. When the floor has been sanded, make up a mixture of glue and wood chips that is thick enough to hold its shape. Use the mixture to fill the gaps between the boards. When the gap filler is dry, sand again and seal the floor.

➡ Check that the glue/sealant you use has low levels of VOCs.

➡ Do not block airbricks in an outside wall as they ventilate the open space beneath the floorboards, which is essential.

SOLID FLOORS

Insulation can be placed on top of concrete floors, followed by whatever flooring is chosen. It's probably best to do this when you are having a major refurbishment as it will raise the floor and may necessitate other work being done (moving electrical sockets etc.). It is always a good idea to insulate beneath any new solid floors, and this is usually a job for a professional.

 WALL INSULATION

Around 35% of the heat loss in a non-insulated home occurs through the walls so find out whether you have wall insulation. There are two options, cavity wall and solid wall insulation, depending on the construction of your house.

CAVITY WALL INSULATION

If your house was built during the last century then the outside walls are probably built in two layers with an air gap or 'cavity' between them. Very often the gap has insulation but, if not, filling the gap between the two layers with an insulating material reduces heat loss through the walls. Cavity wall insulation is not too expensive to install and can be made of various materials, such as mineral wool, foam glass, expanded polystyrene foam (EPS) or urea-formaldehyde foam (avoid the latter if you want to reduce the chemical emissions from your home). It is injected into the cavity from the outside, taking 2–3 hours for a three-bedroom semi-detached house. It costs about £250, and the installers say that it can pay for itself in under two years with the savings made on your heating bills.

In the past there have been some concerns that installing cavity wall insulation increases damp problems. However, over the last 20 years, the process and materials used have improved. All cavity wall insulation installed by a registered contractor is guaranteed against damp problems for 25 years with the Cavity Insulation Guarantee Agency (CIGA), which should provide some protection.

SOLID WALL INSULATION

Some houses have solid walls. This means there is no cavity within the wall to insulate. If you have solid walls you can either insulate them with external or internal insulation.

EXTERNAL INSULATION FOR SOLID WALLS

There are two methods and both may change the external appearance of the property and so can require planning permission.

⬤ Dry cladding offers a wide range of finish materials, including timber panels, stone or clay tiles, brick slips or even aluminium panels.

⬤ External render usually consists of either a sand and cement render applied over a wire mesh, or a thinner, lighter polymer cement render applied over an adhesive 'scrim' layer.

A pebbledash render tends to swallow movement better than a smooth render finish, although it is considered unfashionable in many parts of the UK.

£	TYPE	COST
	External insulation	£10,000 upwards if you do the work at the same time as building work. The energy saving can be up to £400 per year.
	Internal insulation	Starting at £1,200 the energy saving should be around £380 a year.

INTERNAL INSULATION FOR SOLID WALLS

Thermal linings and almost all brands of thermal boarding are very efficient forms of internal insulation. If your walls are in poor condition, it's the perfect time to insulate them, as you end up with smooth new walls. There are two main methods of insulation:

➡ Wooden battens are attached to the wall with insulation fitted between them. The insulation lining is supplied on a roll that is 10mm thick, 1m wide and 12.5m in length. You would then need to cover the insulation with plasterboard and skim the walls or tape and fill the joints to finish.

➡ The all-in-one solution is insulated thermal board, which is fitted directly to the inside of the wall and can be skimmed or joint filled and finished.

TANK AND PIPE INSULATION

A simple and inexpensive way to cut energy loss and save you money, tank and pipe insulation (or lagging) is a must. Both help keep your water hot for longer and prevent pipes freezing in cold weather.

TANK INSULATION

Hot water cylinder jackets can be fitted to your hot water tank and can cut heat loss by up to 75% but they need to be at least 75mm thick in order to achieve these savings. New hot water tanks come fitted with foam insulation.

PIPE INSULATION

Insulating your primary pipes will save you money year on year and is also simple to install. Choose lagging with a minimum thickness of 20mm.

TYPE	COST TO INSTALL	ANNUAL SAVING ON FUEL BILLS	YEARS TO PAY OFF INITIAL OUTLAY
Tank insulation	From £10	£10–15	1 year
Pipe insulation	From £10	Up to £5	2 years

TOP TIPS FOR LAGGING

Cold water pipes in the loft or attic should be insulated too.

Make sure you measure your tank carefully before purchasing a jacket.

Turn off the heating and allow the tank and pipes to cool before you start.

If pipes are not accessible make sure you get help from a plumber.

"If your hot water cylinder is insulated, your hot water will stay hot for longer and you will waste less energy heating it."

SOURCE QUOTE: EDF ENERGY

2

Fixtures and Fittings

ESSENTIAL ELEMENTS

The kitchen and the bathroom are the most fundamental rooms in any house, and the places where having the latest design is highly desirable. In addition these are, potentially, the two most non-environmentally friendly rooms in the house, where the highest proportion of water and energy is used and consumed. So here, we should do what we can to conserve resources, as well as think about using more eco-friendly fixtures and fittings. This includes lighting, a crucial element in the home that rarely has green credentials. However, while we may not want to live like eco-warriors, there are things we can do and simple measures we can take – even changing a standard light bulb. The good news is: the less you use, the better for the environment – and the better for your wallet.

THE GREEN KITCHEN

Kitchens use more energy than anywhere else in the house: the fridge and freezer are always on; the oven, dishwasher and washing machine and tumble drier are in use at different times during the day. It is hardly surprising that the kitchen is the room with the largest carbon footprint in the house. However, it is relatively simple to reduce this footprint.

'REFRESH' NOT 'REMODEL'

Making a kitchen 'green' does not necessarily mean replacing everything you have with eco-friendly alternatives. In fact the greenest approach is actually to try to work as much as possible with what you have already. Repainting and/or replacing cupboard doors or furniture can give you a new look without producing as much waste as fitting a new kitchen.

Units made from particleboard or fibreboard are likely to contain urea formaldehyde and are not resistant to moisture. However, they can be sealed with low-VOC paint or stained, or laminated with a new surface. Additionally, there are a number of companies that can supply you with new doors, which could transform your kitchen without having to have a complete refit.

Generally, unfitted kitchens are an eco-friendly option as they are often made from wood (rather than veneered/melamine chipboard) and units can be moved around and taken with you if you move house. If you have the skill and imagination, you could even make your own using secondhand furniture, with maybe a new worktop.

CHOOSING MATERIALS

While decreasing energy use is the simplest and most effective way of making your kitchen more eco-friendly, you can also choose splashbacks, worktops, units and flooring that have been produced with low environmental impact.

WORKTOPS Today, work surfaces can be made from a wide variety of materials, including recycled paper or hemp, which are durable and easy to clean, but colour selection can be limited. You could opt for for tiles – recycled tiles are available from reclamation yards, as is reclaimed stone or marble. Sustainable wood is a green option, but any new stone, including granite, is a non-renewable resource; once removed from the earth it has gone forever so, from an environmental perspective, it's best avoided.

➡ Use materials that are durable and water-resistant for both worktops and splashbacks so that they will last longer.

➡ If you've used wood for work surfaces, make sure that they are well sealed so they last longer.

UNITS The wood in most kitchen cupboards contains urea-formaldehyde, which releases gases and is believed to be harmful to your health. Look for units made from solid, certified wood, or alternative materials such as bamboo (which is very strong) or wheatboard that use non-toxic finishes. There are a few manufacturers making kitchen units from recycled materials.

FLOORING There is a wide range of eco-friendly flooring available, such as bamboo, cork, real lino and natural rubber. Avoid PVC lino and vinyl, they are among the least green types of flooring (see Flooring page 41–2).

KITCHEN RECYCLING CENTRE

Recycling is becoming easier to do with kerbside collections available in most parts of the country. It can seem like hard work but if you have dedicated bins for different materials this makes recycling easier to organise and quicker to deal with. Recycling collections vary between different local authorities but there will be information available on council websites. You can also take a wider range of items direct to your local recycling centre.

- **RECYCLING BINS** You will probably need about four different bins. They needn't take up much room; there are specially designed bins available but you can just use conventional bins or stackable boxes.

- **PLASTIC** Where they exist, most kerbside schemes currently only accept plastic bottles. Other items such as yoghurt pots and rigid plastic trays can be taken to your recycling centre as they are made from different types of plastic. Old plastic bags can be returned to most supermarkets.

- **GLASS BOTTLES/JARS AND METAL CANS** Accepted in most schemes. Always consider reuse before recycling old jars.

- **PAPER AND CARD** Also included in most kerbside collections. But also see composting (below).

- **COMPOST** This includes any uncooked food waste as well as cardboard and paper. Composting food scraps measn your regular kitchen bin will fill up slowly and won't smell. Hotter, more active compost heaps can also consume tougher stuff like newspaper and paper napkins. If you don't have room in your garden, or it is unsuitable for a compost heap, many Local Authorities offer a kitchen waste collection service.

GREEN MYTHS EXPLORED

DISHWASHERS Although we tend to think that being 'green' is hard work, it's not always the case. You would think that 'doing the dishes' was the eco-friendly option, however, dishwashers, as long as they are fully loaded and set on an eco-efficient cycle, save between three and four times the amount of water used when washing the equivalent by hand, and a substantial amount of energy.

MICROWAVES While some, myself included, are still anxious about the effects of radiation waves from microwaves, to date, there is in fact no actual proof of adverse health effects. They are still an energy-efficient way of cooking (using a great deal less electricity than standard ovens), even if you choose to part cook in the microwave and finish off in the oven.

> " Composting at home for just one year can save global warming gases equivalent to all the CO_2 your kettle produces annually. "

SOURCE QUOTE: RECYCLE NOW

TOP TIPS FOR A GREENER KITCHEN

Replace inefficient appliances with efficient ones when it is time to do so. Avoid energy-guzzling appliances such as huge American-style fridges.

Use your existing appliances efficiently: a clean oven is an efficient one; make sure your fridge is positioned 20cm away from the wall to allow the cooling coils to do their job. Freezers need to be packed tightly.

Use chemical cleaning agents less often or give natural ones a try. Contrary to popular belief most dirt doesn't actually hurt you.

Recycle and compost your rubbish. Recycling bins are quick to install and you can recycle every day.

Use the right sized pan on the right sized hob and turn the heat down when the water has boiled. Cover with a lid – this will help retain heat.

Only boil the water you need in your kettle. De-scale it regularly – it will boil more quickly, saving energy.

YOUR ECO-FRIENDLY KITCHEN

APPLIANCES AND EQUIPMENT

There are two sets of costs to bear in mind when you are choosing appliances – what you pay to take them home and what you pay for the energy and water they use. Kitchen appliances (especially the fridge and the oven) use up most of the energy in the house so it is important to buy on energy ratings. (See pages 92–101 for more details.)

Choose durable, good quality utensils, and pots and pans that will not have to be replaced often. Health (and environmental) concerns surrounding non-stick pans and antibacterial kitchen equipment are very complicated. However, if you are in doubt seek advice from manufacturers and keep it simple – buy products made from natural (renewable and/or sustainable) materials.

GREEN STORAGE SOLUTION

If you happen to buy a property with an old-fashioned pantry or larder, think twice before getting rid of it, or if you have the space, consider building one. It needs to be dark and cool with good ventilation. A walk-in pantry is an eco-friendly option, providing ideal storage space for a wide range of foods that would otherwise be put in the energy-guzzling fridge – eggs, cakes, fruit and vegetables, cooked meats, pickles and so on.

LIVING NATURALLY

'Waste not want not'. Resist 'buy one get one free' – leave the 'free' one in the shop to avoid throwing it in the bin. If you do end up throwing food away, remember that most can be composted.

Making your own food from as natural and local a source as possible will generally be a greener option.

Avoid overpackaged food too; about one third of what we put in the rubbish bin is packaging. Leave as much packaging in the shop, or buy things with less packaging. Reuse foil trays, glass bottles and carrier bags, for instance.

CLEANING

While it is important to keep kitchens clean we do not have to succumb to the vast array of synthetic, chemically charged products that the advertisers would like us to. They are often extremely toxic and mostly are not biodegradable. Instead, choose environmentally friendly, non-toxic products, or make your own with simple ingredients such as soda crystals, white wine vinegar, lemon juice and borax. Try to avoid perfumed products and chlorine bleach, and never use air fresheners.

It's also very easy to make your own cleaning cloths and dusters from old t-shirts.

RECYCLING

We all know the importance of recycling and as the kitchen is the place where most rubbish is generated it makes sense when you are making improvements to your kitchen to think about fitting recycling bins into your kitchen units. (See also page 75.)

THE GREEN BATHROOM

We use – and waste – more water in the bathroom than in any other room in the house. Once you include the energy used to heat the water and the towel rails, and the soaps, shampoos and other detergents, it is easy to see the impact our bathroom has on the environment. However, making your bathroom more eco-friendly is not a daunting task.

SAVING WATER

For a greener bathroom make saving water a priority. Water-efficient loos, showers and taps should be fitted in new bathrooms.

SHOWERS AND BATHS

A shower generally uses a lot less water than a bath, so have a shower rather than a bath (save a bath for a treat). But a power shower is likely to use more water in five minutes than a bath. If you are fitting out a new bathroom, it's important to choose a water-saving shower. Of course, you can always limit your time in the shower.

A typical showerhead delivers 25 litres of water per minute while a low-flow showerhead delivers only 6–15 litres. By using a low-flow showerhead, and you will save a great deal of water.

➡ **AIR SHOWER DEVICES** These can be attached to your existing showerhead. Each water droplet is pumped full of air making it bigger, so it feels the same size as a droplet from a typical showerhead and you use less water. An air shower head can be more expensive than a conventional type – so shop around.

QUICK FIXES FOR YOUR GREEN BATHROOM

Repair dripping taps. A tap dripping at a rate of one drop per second will waste over 12,000 litres of water per year.

Turn off the water while washing, brushing your teeth or shaving – you could save 1,000 litres each week.

Fix leaking loo cisterns. A leaky loo can waste over 2,500 litres of water per month! Place a water-filled 2 litre plastic bottle (or a 'hippo' or 'save a flush' product) in the cistern to reduce the water you use for flushing.

Check that water pipes and external taps are lagged in time for cold winter months. Burst water pipes not only cause serious damage but also waste water.

If you do take a bath, make sure that the plug is in the bath before turning water on. Share a bath – it's fun!

Use natural (biodegradable) body care and cleaning products. Avoid chlorine bleach.

→ **WATER-SAVING SHOWERHEADS** Known as low-flow showers, these have a mechanism that reduces the flow of water but still provides a power-shower feel. Check for models with flow rates (litres per minute) below 15 litres per minute so you can save water.

LOOS

As much as a third of the drinking water that comes into the average home is flushed straight down the loo – a complete waste of a precious resource. You could consider connecting your loo to a rainwater harvesting unit or a grey water system (see pages 146–153). However, these are currently expensive options so think about fitting an efficient water-saving cistern and flush.

Reducing the water used for each flush does represent significant water savings. Ultra-low flow and dual flush loos are available and have improved since they first came onto the market. They can cut household water use by up to 20%. Old cisterns hold about 9 litres of water, whereas new cisterns only hold about 7 litres. Of course, reducing the amount of times you flush saves even more water.

→ **LOO PAPER** You may be using as many as 20,000 sheets of loo paper per year. Do consider using recycled paper and avoid using anti-bacterial wipes as they block the drains.

> " Loos use about 30% of the total water used in a household. "

SOURCE QUOTE: WATERWISE

TAPS

Fix any drips and replace worn tap washers – simple ways of saving water. When fitting new taps use water-saving taps such as push taps, which release water only when pushed and those with a fine spray pattern, minimising water usage.

FITTING A NEW BATHROOM

If you are fitting a completely new bathroom, you have the opportunity to consider other elements such as walls, heating, floors, lighting. It allows you to add more eco-friendly features:

- Make sure that any new walls are well insulated; this will help to reduce the amount of energy you use and your heating bills.

- Consider low-energy-consuming lighting.

- For the floor, consider bamboo, cork, rubber or linoleum – all have green credentials.

Everytime someone fits a brand new bathroom there are usually three large items (bath, loo and basin) that will end up in a landfill site. So if you are fitting a new bathroom, think about the design and choice of sanitaryware very carefully. Make it last – longevity is an important part of being green.

- **RECYCLED MATERIALS** Where possible, it is best to reuse baths and basins or choose secondhand items. You could also consider recycled glass tiles. Glass is completely water-resistant, making it a great choice for bathroom walls and flooring. Recycled ceramic tiles are not so easy to find, but you may find people or builders who will sell off excess stock after a job is finished (check your local Freecycle website), so at least you are not buying new.

YOUR ECO-FRIENDLY BATHROOM

'REFRESH' NOT 'REMODEL'

➡ As with kitchens, making a bathroom 'green' does not mean replacing everything you have with eco-friendly alternatives. In fact, the greenest approach is actually to try to work as much as possible with what you already have. For instance, if you need to replace a cracked basin, you don't necessarily have to replace the bath and loo as well.

➡ And remember, you can fit water-saving devices to existing taps and shower heads.

SALVAGE SOLUTIONS

➡ Consider reclaimed or secondhand fittings instead of buying brand new. Reclaimed taps, tiles and mirrors are also available. They can give your bathroom an individual feel, so see what is available before buying new.

WATER-SAVING HARDWARE

➡ Make sure that you buy water-efficient showers, loos, taps and white goods, if you are fitting a new bathroom or replacing items. It is estimated that if all new homes were built to a water-efficient standard with the installation of water-saving hardware, water consumption could be cut by 20-30% per head.

WINDOWS AND VENTILATION

➡ If possible, a bathroom should have a window for natural light and ventilation. In an eco-friendly bathroom, ideally the window should be double-glazed to help keep the heat in.

➡ Ventilation is important in keeping the room fresh and clean since moist air and surfaces can encourage bacteria and black mould. Open windows, airbricks or vents generally allow adequate ventilation. However, in some instances, an electric extractor is also necessary. If this uses a humidity controller, it will ensure that the fan will run only when it is really needed, limiting the amount of electricity that is used, although these can be a little unreliable. New bathrooms require extractor fans to comply with building regulations.

BATHROOM ACCESSORIES

➡ We should be aware of how we decorate and use the bathroom on a daily basis. For example, choose a bamboo rather than vinyl bath mat, an organic cotton rather than a plastic shower curtain, and try to buy soaps and shampoos with fewer or no man-made chemicals. The choices we make can help reduce or increase the damage done to the environment.

➡ In addition, as in the kitchen, we should limit the use of bathroom cleaning products that are not environmentally friendly.

➡ Lighting in the bathroom can be low but with a more intense light near the mirror for make-up and shaving. Use white energy-saving bulbs.

LIGHT SOURCES

According to a report published by the International Energy Agency (IEA), a global switch to efficient lighting systems would cut the world's electricity bill by nearly 10%. But the situation is perhaps not quite as clear as many reports imply.

WHAT CAN WE DO?

On a domestic level, nearly one third of our annual electricity bill or an average of £150 per year is spent on lighting. So how do we make our lighting more energy-efficient? We can either maximise natural light or save electricity.

DAYLIGHT TUBES

A way to introduce natural light in darker spaces is to install light pipes: tube day lighting systems that take daylight from the rooftop and pipe it through highly reflective tubing to where it's needed (see opposite). They make dark landings and entrance halls less reliant on artificial lighting during the day.

HOW MUCH DO THEY COST? The tubes cost about £250. The cost of installation will depend on how long the tube needs to be – some homes need the light to travel from the roof to the basement, which will be more than the cost of lighting the upstairs landing, for example. Talk to your builder before you buy.

WHAT ARE THE BENEFITS? Once fitted there are no other costs. They provide increased day light thus saving on electric light.

SOURCE QUOTE: NHS DIRECT

HOW MUCH WORK IS REQUIRED? In an existing house you will need to make a hole in your roof and ceilings in order to fit the tube. New builds can really benefit from this type of system.

> **Sunlight helps you to produce vitamin D, and can alleviate the symptoms of depression, especially during winter months.**

DAYLIGHT TUBE

This unique dome and tubing system is suitable for virtually all pitched and flat roofs. Natural light is reflected into the 305mm long tubes and delivered into a dark room through the diffuser, which fits neatly to the ceiling.

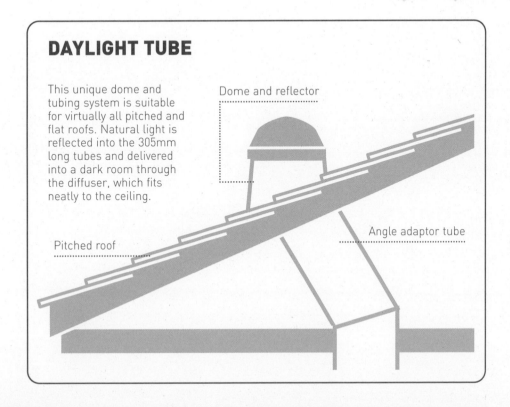

Dome and reflector

Pitched roof

Angle adaptor tube

LIGHT QUALITY

Light quality affects how well people can see to do tasks and how visually comfortable they feel. If you want to save money, consider the three categories of lighting available to you, and don't light a wider area than you actually need.

➡ Ambient lighting is background lighting and used for doing general things around the house.

➡ Task lighting provides sufficient light for tasks to be completed accurately, such as reading, but not so much light that entire areas are illuminated.

➡ Accent lighting is used to illuminate certain areas that you want to blend more closely with bright areas such as windows.

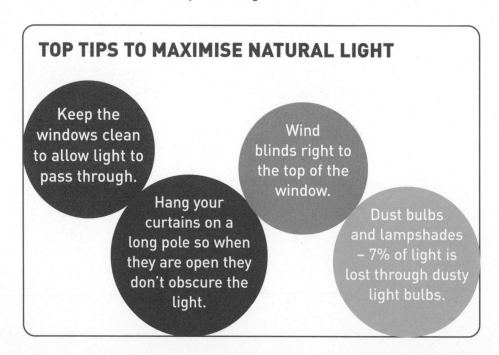

TOP TIPS TO MAXIMISE NATURAL LIGHT

Keep the windows clean to allow light to pass through.

Hang your curtains on a long pole so when they are open they don't obscure the light.

Wind blinds right to the top of the window.

Dust bulbs and lampshades – 7% of light is lost through dusty light bulbs.

THE LIGHT BULB (LAMP) DEBATE

▶ **REPLACE STANDARD BULBS** Research by Greenpeace UK suggests that by changing to energy-efficient light bulbs you could make an average 15% saving on electricity costs, or around £50 per year.

▶ **SWITCH THEM OFF** If you have a large family now is the time to teach them to switch off the lights when they leave the room. Make it a habit to walk round the house before you go to bed switching everything off.

INCANDESCENT BULBS

Nearly one third of our electricity bills is spent on lighting. Incandescent bulbs (the classic filament design) have changed very little since their invention in 1879. They use more power on a second by second basis but are more environmentally friendly to manufacture and dispose of. Additionally, incandescent bulbs are more likely to be turned off as they light up instantly, whereas low-energy bulbs are not designed to be turned on and off.

COMPACT FLUORESCENT BULBS (CFLS)

These are generally more expensive than incandescent bulbs but require far less energy to produce the same amount of light and can last up to twelve times as long (10,000 hours). The downsides are that they are slow to light, which means that they are more often left on and, as fluorescent has a slight blue tinge, it is a fairly unpleasant light to live with. Be aware that many of the claims on the packaging do not take into consideration the full energy consumption of a CFL bulb. There are far more components in a CFL bulb including mercury, which is a hazard if not disposed of very carefully.

HOW MUCH DO THEY COST? Like many green alternatives, initial outlay is often significantly more than the traditional product. The Energy Saving Trust compared a standard 100W bulb and its equivalent 18W CFL bulb. They calculated a potential lifetime saving (10,000 hours) of up to £60 and suggest that the average user can save £45 per year by switching to CFLs, with a payback time of under two years. Of course, you may have the incandescent bulb on for less time due to heat up time but there is clear financial saving there.

As a general rule you pay for what you get with all bulbs and it is worth paying extra for quality.

PROBLEMS WITH CFL BULBS

➡ Dimmer switches – Some class A (for savings) standard CFLs cannot cope with the change in voltage caused by dimmer switches and they flicker. However, dimmer-proof CFLs have been developed. They are expensive, but as the technology improves, prices are likely to come down.

➡ Disposal – Energy-saving bulbs contain a small amount of mercury, which is highly toxic. Although most local councils still don't offer CFL recycling, don't be tempted to just bin them. Thankfully, there are a number of shops that will recycle them.

"In March 2007, the government announced it would ban incandescent bulbs by 2011. This should lead to improved recycling facilities by local councils to cope with the increase of CFLs."

SOURCE QUOTE: FRIENDS OF THE EARTH

LIGHT EMITTING DIODES (LEDS)

Rather more efficient and more pleasant than CFLs, LEDs reduce electricity consumption by 80–90% and last up to 100,000 hours. They even light up faster than regular bulbs. However, the drawback is that they don't work with dimmer switches.

LEDs contain a phosphor tube that glows when it is charged. There is no filament to burn out and switching on or off does not reduce the lamp lifetime. And, because they last so long, you will spend much less time replacing them. As yet, there are still problems with LEDs and light dimmers – talk to your electrician, because if you place at least one incandescent bulb in the circuit, then the dimmers can be made to work effectively. LED light is not very powerful or strong, and so is good for backlighting, but less attractive for focused lighting.

➡ Expected to last 10 years at 3 hours a day

➡ Five times brighter than traditional bulbs

➡ 80% less power consumption

CERAMIC METAL HALIDE

Currently mainly used in industrial and commercial environments, these bulbs are highly efficient and give off a more pleasing light than CFL bulbs.

DIY LIGHTING

Lighting is not just about the bulbs but about the fixtures and fittings as well. Keep your eyes open for lamps you like the look of in discount or antique shops.

GREEN APPLIANCES

We use a wide range of energy-guzzling appliances in our homes – ovens, fridges, dishwashers, washing machines and tumble dryers – as well as other electrical goods, such as televisions and DVD players. For the most part, we rely on them and would not want to be without them. However, there are ways of saving money and energy. Today, due to the fact that Eco labelling and the Energy Star certification has come into operation in Europe (and other parts of the world), the vast majority of manufacturers produce appliances that take water and energy consumption into consideration.

SWITCH THEM OFF

One of the easiest eco-friendly things you can do is to switch appliances off standby when you have finished using them: it is estimated that £875 million worth of energy is wasted in the UK every year by appliances left on standby.

BUY ENERGY-EFFICIENT APPLIANCES

There are different rating systems to look out for when purchasing new appliances.

▶ **THE ENERGY SAVING TRUST** has a scheme which recommends products that meet strict criteria on energy efficiency. The criteria are set by an independent panel and reviewed annually. 'A' is the highest rating. Only the most efficient products also carry the Energy Saving Recommended logo which promises that these products have met the strict criteria on energy efficiency, will cost less to run and help reduce carbon emissions.

▶ **THE EU ENERGY LABEL** rates products from A (the most efficient) to G (the least efficient). By law, the label must be shown on all refrigeration appliances, electric tumble dryers, washing machines, washer dryers, dishwashers, electric ovens, air conditioners, lamps and light bulb packaging.

Some appliances are given double-A or even triple-A ratings. This is because they have two or three different energy-using functions that need to be measured.

WASHING MACHINES can be rated A for energy consumption, A for wash quality and A for spin.

TUMBLE DRIERS are energy inefficient and you are unlikely to find one with an A-rating for energy consumption

FRIDGES a new EU Directive has a revised criteria of A+ for fridges.

EU ENERGY LABEL

The EU Energy Label provides clear, recognisable information about the energy consumption and performance of products and by law, must be attached to appliances displayed for sale. An important part of the label is the colour-coded rating scale, which provides a simple index of the product's efficiency from 'A' (the most efficient) to 'G' (the least efficient).

ENERGY SAVING RECOMMENDED LOGO

The Energy Saving Recommended logo is carried by products that meet strict criteria on energy efficiency.

Energy
Washing machine

Manufacturer
Model

More efficient

| A |
| B |
| C |
| D |
| E |
| F |
| G |

B

Less efficient

Energy consumption kWh/cycle	**1.75**
(based on standard test results for 60°C cotton cycle)	
Actual energy consumption will depend on how the appliance is used	
Washing performance	**A** BCDEFG
A: higher G: lower	
Spin drying performance	A**B**CDEFG
A: higher G: lower	
Spin speed (rpm)	1400
Capacity (cotton) kg	5.0
Water consumption	5.5
Noise Washing	5.2
(dB(A) re 1 pW) Spinning	7.6
Further information contained in product brochure	

POTENTIAL SAVINGS

If you look for 'A'-rated appliances you could make significant savings. The savings detailed here assume replacing an average appliance purchased new in 1995 with an Energy Saving Recommended model of similar size and and electricity cost of 10p/kWh. So think twice before chucking out perfectly good working appliances.

APPLIANCE	EU ENERGY RATING	SAVING A YEAR (UP TO)	CO_2 SAVING A YEAR (UP TO)
Fridge-freezer	A+ or A++	£37	148 kg
Upright or Chest Freezer	A+ or A++	£27	109 kg
Refrigerator	A+ or A++	£16	64 kg
Washing machine	A	£8	42 kg
Dishwasher	A	£16	85 kg
Integrated digital televisions	–	£5	20 kg

"Buying the most energy-efficient option will save you money in the long run."

WASHING MACHINES

Your washing machine is a massive energy consumer (whatever the size of the drum) – most machines run an average of 274 cycles a year. You can save energy by:

➡ Washing at lower temperatures. Washing clothes at 30°C instead of a higher temperature can use around 40% less electricity.

➡ Using a detergent that works effectively at a lower temperature.

➡ A full load is an easy energy saver. Where this isn't possible, use a half load or economy programme.

➡ An energy-efficient machine could cut your energy consumption by up to one third. With a washing machine you are looking for a triple A (AAA) rating: A for energy, A for wash quality and A for spin.

£200-1,000 to buy new

SAVING If you use your washing machine three times a week at a cost of 40p per load you will be saving an estimated £20 a year in your energy bills by switching to an energy-efficient model.

TUMBLE DRYERS

Tumble dryers are not energy-efficient. Most tumble dryers are C-rated. If they use condensers they move up to a B. There are tumble dryers with an A rating but these models run overnight and do not use heat, just air, to dry a load. The solution is, where possible, try not to use one, or use infrequently when you need to dry something very quickly.

WHEN USING A TUMBLE DRYER

➡ Remember to use the high spin speed on your washing machine to get your washing really dry.

➡ Use maximum load in your tumble dryer every time.

➡ Keep the filter clean of those bits of fluff that stop the hot air circulating.

C rated £100–600 to buy new
B rated £275–350 to buy new

SAVING Using a tumble dryer is never energy efficient.

SAVING MONEY ON WASHING AND DRYING

If you do use a tumble dryer, check the dryer vent – don't let it get blocked.

Wash and dry full loads.

Don't over-dry your clothes – they are easier to fold when they are still slightly damp, and this saves time and money on ironing.

Heating the water uses about 90% of a washing machine's energy, so use cooler water. Switching from hot to warm can cut a load's energy use in half and will still do a good job of cleaning your clothes.

Traditional drying methods cannot be beaten so, if possible, use washing lines (rotary lines take up very little space) or clothes airers. Consider fitting a 'Sheila maid' – an old-fashioned drying rack, which is hoisted up close to the ceiling to be in the hottest part of the room.

DISHWASHERS

It costs around half as much to run a cycle on an energy-saving dishwasher as it does on an inefficient machine, so it is definitely worth looking out for the top rating when you next upgrade.

- An Energy Saving Recommended dishwasher uses less water and 40% less energy. Always look for the logo (see page 94).

- If your water is metered, you'll also save money by using less water per wash cycle.

£200-500 to buy new

SAVING If you use your dishwasher every day at a cost of 40p per load you will be saving an estimated £58 in your energy bills each year by switching to an energy-efficient model.

> **If everyone in the UK replaced their old dishwasher with an Energy Saving Recommended model, £40 million a year would be saved and 170,000 tonnes of CO_2.**

SOURCE QUOTE: ENERGY SAVING TRUST

FRIDGES AND FREEZERS

Fridges and freezers are always on and continuously using electricity, so if your fridge or freezer is energy-efficient it will cost you less in the long run. Energy Saving Recommended fridges and fridge-freezers use at least 60% less energy than older models. For refrigeration the EU energy label goes up to A++.

Until you need to change your existing fridge or freezer:

➡️ Try to keep the thermostat at a low level.

➡️ Don't let it fill up with ice so that it has to work even harder.

➡️ Make sure that your fridge is 20cm away from the wall (to allow the coils to work efficiently).

DISPOSAL It is estimated that up to three million domestic refrigeration units (fridges, fridge-freezers and freezers) are disposed of in the UK each year. Fridges manufactured before 1994 used chlorofluorocarbons (CFCs) and hydrochlorofluorocarbons (HCFCs) that were linked to damage to the ozone layer. Modern fridges are generally manufactured using HFC (R134a) or hydrocarbon (HC600a) refrigerants and hydrocarbon blowing agents, which are generally less expensive. Although less damaging than CFCs, both substances deplete the ozone layer, and so have to be removed before the appliances are scrapped. This requirement came into force for domestic appliances from 1 January 2002. Local authorities are obliged to accept refrigerators or freezers from households at a civic site free of charge. They are also obliged to provide a collection service for bulky household items, although they can charge for collection.

Buying the smallest fridge or freezer that meets your needs can make a big difference. Even when they are both A rated, a typical larger-sized American-style fridge-freezer uses a lot more energy than a standard fridge-freezer.

OVENS

When choosing a new oven the type of power that you use should be taken into consideration in terms of its green credentials. Gas is generally regarded as a greener choice than electricity for cooking as it has lower climate change effects. However, microwaves are more energy efficient than gas or electric ovens (see page 76), and electric induction hobs do match the energy efficiency of gas hobs. Electric ovens are covered by the European Energy label so look for one with the highest energy efficiency rating (gas ovens are not covered by the scheme but are still the greenest choice).

Assuming you have bought three new appliances at a total mid-range price of £1,350 for an Energy Saving Recommended dishwasher, fridge-freezer and washing machine, your annual savings will be an estimated £166 per year. If your appliances last ten years and the price of energy continues to rise then you will be saving money as well as energy.

ELECTRICAL EQUIPMENT

As well as household appliances we are also using an increasing variety of gadgets. Every year in the UK, we spend more than £12 billion on items such as television sets, games consoles and home entertainment equipment, making us Europe's biggest consumers in this sector.

STANDBY

Around 8% of total energy consumption from television use is from standby alone, so turn it off when you have finished watching and save yourself money. If you are buying new check that the item in question has a manual 'off' switch. Some do not so you would need to use the wall switch to turn them off.

> "£875 million worth of energy is wasted in the UK every year by people leaving appliances on standby."

SOURCE QUOTE: ENERGY SAVING TRUST

CHOOSING ELECTRONIC EQUIPMENT

☑ Do some research before you shop. Look for products that are energy efficient: a flat screen television can cost up to three times as much to run as a traditional television. This can add up to £85 to a typical household electricity bill every year.

☑ Look for the logo. The Energy Saving Recommended logo (see page 94) is a easy way to find the most energy-efficient products.

☑ Ask in-store. With energy consumption continuing to rise, the running costs and efficiency of a product are important considerations. Questions to ask:

➡ How much energy does the product use when on standby?

➡ Does the product have any special energy-efficient features such as automatic standby?

☑ Look out for integrated appliances. Fewer products means less electricity, so buying an integrated digital television for instance, which combines a television with a digital receiver, is good for both your pocket and the environment.

☑ Reuse – think carefully before buying new – the greenest thing you can do is to keep using what you have or buy second hand.

TELEVISIONS

☑ Flat screen LCD televisions are high-energy users, and also use an industrial chemical in their production called nitrogen trifluoride, which is 17,000 times more potent than carbon dioxide as a greenhouse gas.

☑ The latest integrated digital televisions (IDTVs) receive digital television without the need for a set-top box. With the digital switchover due to take place by 2012, it is a good time to think of switching to an Energy Saving Recommended IDTV.

☑ IDTVs perform the same function as a television plus a set-top box but use just one power supply rather than two.

☑ Unlike many set-top boxes IDTVs can be switched off without losing their settings and so do not have to be left on standby.

£	PRICE RANGE FOR DIGITAL TVS	COST
	Basic – 19"	*c.* £180
	Mid-range – 19" + DVD	*c.* £230
	High-end range – 22" + DVD	from £300

SET-TOP BOXES The switch to digital television will affect all households by 2012. Once your region has undergone the switchover every television set will need to be compatible with a digital signal to be able to receive broadcasts.

➡ If you are planning to replace your TV set, you can buy an Integrated Digital TV (IDTV) which has the digital receiver built in (see above).

➡ If you are not planning to replace your television in the near future, you can convert your existing set to receive a digital signal by purchasing a set-top box. These are widely available from electrical retailers, and are compatible with the vast majority of television sets, even black-and-white models.

➡ Energy Saving Recommended set-top boxes are measured on both standby and on-mode power consumption to ensure they are among the most energy efficient products on the market.

➡ An Energy Saving Recommended standard set-top box consumes 50% less electricity than a typical set-top box and therefore will cost half as much to run.

SOURCE QUOTE: ENERGY SAVING TRUST

"Experts say that by 2020 consumer electronics and information communication technology are expected to account for nearly half of all domestic energy use."

COMPUTER GAMES CONSOLES

The latest generation of computer games consoles consume up to an astonishing 180W of electricity – the equivalent of leaving three 60W bulbs burning, and potentially adding £160 per year to the electricity bill. There are many reasons to limit your child's use of computer games, so add this one to the list!

DIGITAL RADIOS

DAB (Digital Audio Broadcasting) radios work by converting traditional analogue signals into a digital format prior to transmission. Digital radios have been one of the biggest-selling consumer electronic products over the last five years. Digital radios usually use more power than their analogue equivalents. That is because they switch into standby when turned 'off' and so go on using energy unless you switch them off at the socket.

TOP TIPS WHEN BUYING A COMPUTER

Energy Star is a label that guarantees energy efficiency – it should save £20 a year in energy over the lifetime of a PC or printer compared to a machine without the label.

Understand how the sleep mode can be enabled on the machine so you don't leave it on all the time

New digital high-tech electronic equipment is not yet as energy-efficient as appliances – but it's only a matter of time.

Laptops use 70% less energy than desktop computers.

FINISHING TOUCHES

Whether you have been refurbishing a new house or have been redecorating a room in your home, try to introduce eco-friendly elements when you are planning the finishing touches – including soft furnishings, wallpaper, furniture and tableware. When we buy furnishings we are often persuaded by instant appeal or trends and cost. Mostly, we don't find out about where it comes from, what it is made of, or how long it will last. And there are no clear guidelines to help us decide whether products are eco-friendly.

GREEN CRITERIA

When you start looking for finishing touches try to find products that meet the following green criteria:

- Aim to reduce your material consumption – think about whether you will like it a few years' time, and make sure it is well-made and long-lasting.

- Secondhand or antique items are well worth considering.

- Produced in the UK, ideally near where you live. This supports your local community and avoids the necessity for high energy imports. Pay a fair price for Fairtrade, if you choose to buy imported goods.

- Grown from sustainable or renewable material, for instance, FSC-certified wood.

- Created organically or at least without toxic chemicals.

▶ Made from recycled materials – remember, you can reuse materials found in your home, and repair furniture rather than throw it away.

SOFT FURNISHINGS AND BEDDING

Basically, soft furnishings fall into two categories: those made from natural and those made from synthetic materials. Generally, fabrics are pretty innocuous; however, it's worth considering how different fibres affect your health, and the pollution created by the production processes and the dyes. A little thought can go a long way; every little bit helps to keep the planet clean. Consider the following options.

FABRICS

▶ Natural fabrics, such as wool and organic cotton (see cotton below), are mostly made from renewable materials and are a popular eco-friendly choice because they are long lasting, breathe well, don't create static electricity and are relatively non-allergenic. Although synthetic fabrics, such as polyester and acrylic are hard wearing, they attract dust and do not breathe as well as natural fibres. Plus the fact that most synthetic fabrics, from curtain fabrics to bed linens, are treated with chemicals during and after processing.

▶ Conventionally grown cotton is the world's most polluting crop, and nearly one quarter of all insecticides produced globally are used on cotton plants. Unlike conventionally grown fibres, organic fibres are grown without the use of synthetic chemicals to promote growth and deter pests. Organic cotton duvet covers, pillowcases and towels are available. Look for organic labelling (Soil Association in the UK).

In addition to organic cotton, you can choose hemp, cruelty-free silk and recycled-plastic fleece. An alternative to cotton derived from bamboo is also available. It is naturally antiallergenic and three times as absorbent as cotton.

FILLINGS

In addition to the fabric, you should consider the green credentials of the fillings (natural and synthetic) used in cushions, upholstery or bedding. Duck and goose feathers are inexpensive and long lasting; however, duck down is warmer but more expensive. Down is collected in the moulting season, technically making it a more ethical and ecological filling, as feathers are often collected from the slaughter house. Some people have an allergic reaction to feathers, so rely on synthetic fillings (acrylic and polyester) to provide hypo-allergenic alternatives. If possible, avoid foam chips and blocks as they are treated with fire-retardant chemicals and are not biodegradable.

Mattresses can be made from 100% natural, organic material as well, such as Welsh wool.

RUGS AND FITTED CARPETS

The advantage of a rug is that it is easy to change the look of a room and, as carpets harbour more dirt, some people find rugs more hygienic. In terms of heating costs, fitted carpets win the environmental argument hands down. If you opt for fitted carpets it's best to choose a wool or wool mix. Even so, some are chemically treated to reduce staining. If you have a choice, avoid synthetic carpets: although they are cheaper, they are made from a variety of petrochemically derived fibres that use high-energy processes and produce toxins. Either way a good vacuum cleaner (such as a Vorwerk) will make your carpets last longer and remove more mites, which can cause allergies.

➡ It's a good idea to look after your rugs, carpets and upholstery. By keeping furnishings clean it will help them last longer.

WALL COVERINGS

Generally, wallpaper is an eco-friendly material, being made mainly from wood pulp (from sustainable or recycled sources). If possible, avoid vinyl wallpaper which is paper covered with a film of pvc.

➡ Look out for greener wallpaper, which uses recycled FSC-certified paper with solvent-free ink.

➡ Glasstex is a glass-fibre material applied like wallpaper. It is made from natural, non-toxic materials such as quartz, soda, lime and dolomite. It comes in textures such as fine linen, coarse twisted or fluffy yarns, for subtle or rustic effects.

FURNITURE

Before buying furniture, bear in mind the eco-friendly mantra – reduce, reuse, then recycle.

➡ Choose new furniture made using timber from sustainable forests or FSC-certified wood (see pages 20–1).

➡ If you have the choice, go for solid wood rather than veneers. Solid wood can be painted, or resanded and finished. Veneered products are difficult to repair and are not as long lasting.

➤ Remember to take care of wooden furniture (wax it or seal it and remove water or any stains quickly) – so that it ages well.

➤ Consider buying items that are multifunctional and adaptable. One item can sometimes do the job of two – such as sofa beds, or dining tables with drop-down leaves.

➤ Buy secondhand or antique furniture. Try reclaimed furniture suppliers or local recycling message boards or auction sites.

➤ Metal furniture – the energy required to mine iron is far greater than the energy needed to harvest wood (aluminium is even higher). If you choose metal objects, look after them.

TABLEWARE

As well as considering secondhand or antique items, choose from a wide range of green materials including:

➤ Recycled glass reduces the need to extract more raw materials.

➤ Stainless steel (an alloy of iron) is long-lasting and easy to recycle, but remember that iron requires intensive energy to extract, and is becoming a increasingly rare metal. So if, for example, you are buying stainless steel cutlery, choose carefully so that you can use it indefinitely.

➤ Biodegradable plastics are gradually becoming available. While conventional plastics are made from oil and do not degrade, biodegradable plastics are made from plants.

3

Powering
the Home

ENERGY RESERVES

Energy resources such as coal and oil are scarce and getting scarcer. As well as making our energy use more efficient, governments and individuals are now committed to investigating ways of minimising the use of fossil fuels and making greater use of sustainable energy sources, for instance solar or wind power.

WHAT WILL HAPPEN IN THE FUTURE?

Governments are only too aware of the problems that the current reliance on fossil fuels brings, both from a political and environmental point of view. In addition, international protocols on clean air and commitments to the reduction of carbon emissions, have encouraged an increased emphasis on the exploitation of renewable sources of energy, and this will only continue.

LIFETIMES OF EARTH'S ENERGY RESERVES

Coal: 165–285 years at current use (estimates vary)

Natural gas: about 60 years at current use

Oil: about 40 years at current use

SOURCES OF ELECTRICITY

ENERGY SOURCE	PERCENTAGE
Gas	39.93
Coal	33.08
Nuclear	19.26
Renewables (solar, wind and water power)	3.55
Hydroelectric	1.1
Imports	1.96
Oil	1.12

SOURCE: BERR (DEPARTMENT FOR BUSINESS ENTERPRISE & REGULATORY REFORM

CONTROLLING ENERGY

Controlling energy usage is the first and most important step in reducing your carbon footprint. If you study your daily routine you can produce an energy schedule that might help to identify high-energy points in the day. You can then decide how energy savings can be made and build them into your routine. For example, not running the dishwasher and washing machine until you have a full load, or turning off the television or computer when you leave the room. When you are aware of your routine you can decide what you think will be easiest to control.

ENERGY COMPANIES

Energy companies are increasingly using sustainable energy (biofuels, geothermal power and tidal power) as part of their energy supply. It is now possible to choose greener energy options through your supplier. In the home you can have your own sustainable power source based on power from the wind, sun, heat in the ground or biofuels. Even if we reduced our carbon footprint by as little as 10%, we would be making huge savings, not only for our monthly bills, but for global health as well.

UNDERSTAND YOUR BILLS

It also helps to understand your energy bills, but this is often easier said than done. In a recent survey, energy bills were regarded as the most difficult to understand of all household bills; indeed, 82% of people in Britain didn't know which energy tariff had been selected from their energy supplier or the actual amount they were paying for gas and electricity! The research, commissioned by the Energy Saving Trust, found that almost half of respondents would be interested in having a smart meter (see page 118).

ENERGY TARIFFS

There are various options for energy tariffs, such as fixed or variable pricing deals on gas and electricity, discounted deals where you buy your gas and electricity from the same supplier, or green energy tariffs where the supplier pledges to use energy from sustainable or renewable sources. (See also page 119.)

SMART METERS

These allow householders to monitor how much their energy costs the environment and their pocket. They can also tell instantly which household appliances cost the most money to run and the times of day when it is more expensive to use them. Smart meters have been in use in Italy since 2005 and energy use has dropped 5% per year. Trials are currently being conducted across the UK but there is a debate over how and when a national rollout should occur. It is possible to buy smart meters in the UK and trials have shown that householders who use them tend to reduce their energy bills by 5–10%. For a four-person family living in a three-bedroom house with energy bills totalling £1,000 a year, this represents a saving of up to £100. However, many meters are complicated to use and understand. Being more aware of the amount of energy you are using makes it much easier to make savings.

NUCLEAR ENERGY

Energy companies now also use nuclear power, which many believe to be the solution to fossil fuels running out. However, it is made from uranium which needs to be mined overseas, which means we are still not energy independent. It is efficient in some ways because a very small amount of uranium creates a vast amount of power, but the waste created in the process cannot be disposed of properly and causes huge problems.

GREEN ELECTRICITY

Most electricity in the UK is generated by burning coal and gas in power stations, which releases carbon dioxide into the atmosphere. While nuclear power produces no carbon emissions, the waste materials do create environmental problems. The government has targeted a 60% reduction of CO_2 emissions by 2050. It has established key proposals, such as the Renewables Obligation, which is boosting investment and installations by forcing electricity suppliers to source an increasing percentage of electricity from renewable sources.

GREEN ELECTRICITY is defined as electricity produced from sources that do not produce carbon dioxide or have other harmful effects on the environment in the ways explained above.

GREEN POWER OPTIONS

Electricity companies do offer customers a green power option on their bill. Signing up for green power usually means paying more, but if you are committed, you might be prepared to make this change. Be aware that only certain companies actually invest in creating more green energy. Many simply use the green energy off the grid that has been made anyway. However, a few electricity companies actually invest in green energy, adding weight to the growth of wind farms. We should encourage them by signing up for green power.

- There are energy-supplier switching websites that deal exclusively with green electricity tariffs. Be careful to choose the right one.

- Exploring green power options is a good introduction to renewable energy and will inspire more complex energy solutions.

SUSTAINABLE ENERGY SOURCES

When energy is sustainable it can be produced economically and safely for all time without impacting on the environment and well-being of future generations. As governments begin to make a great commitment to finding sustainable and renewable sources of energy, what can we do to help the environment and save money?

PHOTOVOLTAIC SOLAR POWER

Solar energy is converted to electricity using Photovoltaic (PV) technology. PV cells work by using solar cells to convert light from the sun into direct current (DC) electricity. It is the light energy, and not the heat from the sun, that creates the power source in PV systems. PV cells are referred to in terms of the energy they would generate operating in full sunlight, known as a kilowatt peak (kWp).

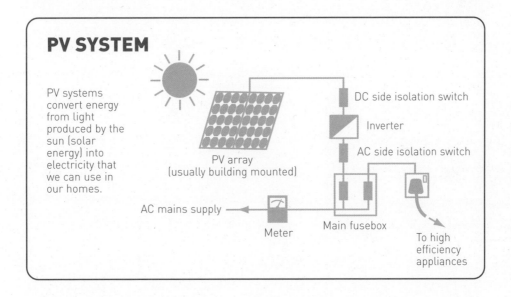

PV SYSTEM

PV systems convert energy from light produced by the sun (solar energy) into electricity that we can use in our homes.

PV array
(usually building mounted)

DC side isolation switch

Inverter

AC side isolation switch

AC mains supply

Meter

Main fusebox

To high efficiency appliances

SOLAR PANELS The electrical output from a single PV cell is small, so several cells are connected together to form a panel. Depending on your energy needs a number of panels can be connected together to give the required electrical output. The DC electricity produced is fed into an inverter that converts it into AC electricity, which is mains voltage compatible and can be used in the home.

STORAGE You can store your electricity in batteries, but it is probably better to ensure your system is 'grid-connected' so that when you are not generating enough of your own electricity you can tap into the national grid. Conversely, if you are producing more than you need, you can sell the excess back to your energy supplier.

 The cost of a fully installed PV system depends upon the size of the system and how it is mounted. As a general guideline, a solar PV system typically costs £5,000–7,500 per kWp installed. Most domestic systems are usually between 1.5 and 3kWp.

IS MY HOME SUITABLE? To maximise the efficiency of a solar PV system, a property will require an obstruction-free roof slope of between 30 and 45 degrees from horizontal, with an area of at least 10 sq m that faces between south east and south west. The roof slope should be free from shadows that may be cast by other parts of the building or nearby buildings or trees. Any manufacturer will be able to advise when they come to quote.

➡ Caution – solar panels are heavy and your roof must be strong enough to hold the weight.

DO I NEED PLANNING PERMISSION? All homeowners in England are, generally, able to install microgeneration equipment, such as solar panels, without needing to get planning permission, as long as there is clearly no impact on others. However, in some instances, you may need planning consent. This usually applies to listed buildings or those in a conservation area, but it is always recommended that you check with your local planning authority first. Householders in Wales, Scotland and Northern Ireland must consult with their local authority, too.

ARE GRANTS AVAILABLE?

Through the Low Carbon Buildings Programme, the government offers householders the opportunity to take advantage of grants to help them purchase and install microgeneration equipment. You could get up to £2,500 in rebates, but there are certain criteria that must be met in order for you to be eligible.

HOW MUCH WILL I SAVE?

An average 2.5kWp set-up can generate around 50% of a household's needs, or save you around £230 per year, depending on how much you pay for your electricity. Solar power is expensive to install but manufacturers say it could save up to 45% of your energy bills.

HOW LONG WILL IT LAST?

Guaranteed to be up to 80% effective for 25 years; could last longer.

£	RATING (KW)	NO OF PANELS	COST	ANNUAL ELECTRICITY BILL	% SAVING ON ANNUAL ELECTRICITY BILL	YEARS TO RECOUP INITIAL OUTLAY
	1.4	8	£8,640	£460	28%	47 yrs
	2.1	12	£11,800	£460	42%	49 yrs
	2.8	16	£14,400	£460	56%	46 yrs

WIND POWER

The potential for wind power is immense. The most comprehensive study to date found that wind power on land and near-shore could be harnessed to equal 54,000 million tonnes of oil per year, or over five times the world's current energy use in all its forms. However, there is a limit to using wind power since the resource available is far larger than any practical means to develop it. But can all this potential be adapted to the home?

HOW DOES IT WORK? Turbines use the force of the wind to turn a rotor that produces electricity. Systems that are not connected to the national grid require batteries to store the electricity and an inverter to convert the DC electricity to AC (alternating current) power that can be used in the home. Systems can also be connected to the national grid and a special inverter used to convert the electricity at a standard suitable for the grid, meaning no battery is necessary. Unused or excess electricity can be sold to the local supply company (although at a lower figure than the cost of producing the electricity).

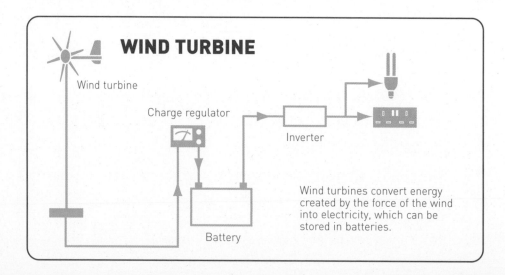

WIND TURBINE

Wind turbine

Charge regulator

Inverter

Battery

Wind turbines convert energy created by the force of the wind into electricity, which can be stored in batteries.

Many small turbines struggle to produce a worthwhile amount of energy and certainly not enough to power the whole home. At some point in the future there should be smaller turbines that work well, but for now remember the green mantra 'reduce' and think carefully before buying a wind turbine that may not be effective.

TYPES OF WIND TURBINES:

➤ Mast mounted – these are free standing and located near the building(s) that will be using the electricity.

➤ Roof mounted – these can be installed on house roofs and other buildings, although they are not generally advisable.

IS MY HOME SUITABLE? Suitability will be determined by the intended use of the power supply: small turbines can power battery-charging systems while larger ones can supply power to the national grid. An ideal site is flat, high ground, free from obstructions.

➤ Windspeed increases with height so site the turbine as high as possible.

➤ Check with the British Wind Energy Association website to find out how much wind is generated in your area, and obtain a professional assessment of the windspeed at the proposed location over a period of time before going ahead and installing a wind turbine.

DO I NEED PLANNING PERMISSION? You do need planning permission for a wind turbine of any real use. You must also consult your neighbours – one man in Essex had to fight 22 planning objections to get his turbine installed, and he is not alone.

HOW MUCH DOES IT COST?

The most basic, roof-mounted system can cost as little as £500. This includes a turbine, rigging, cable, regulator, battery and inverter. However, this may only generate enough power to light the energy-saving light bulbs in your home, if that, although the manufacturers do boast that you can accumulate energy in the battery to run more electrical equipment at non-peak times. At the other end of the scale, installing a 10m turbine generating 2.5–6kW can cost £11,000–19,000. As well as installation the costs include turbine, mast, inverters and battery storage.

ARE GRANTS AVAILABLE? Grants of up to £2,500 are available through the Low Carbon Buildings Programme. You will need to use a certified installer and products.

HOW MUCH WILL I SAVE? Data is currently being collected on potential savings of energy and carbon. Savings depend on many factors including size and location of the turbine, windspeed, obstructions and local landscape.

HOW LONG WILL IT LAST? The equipment is guaranteed to last more than 20 years with regular service checks.

RATING (KW)	COST	GRANT
1kw	£1,500	up to £1,000
2.5kw	£11,000	£2,500
6kw	£19,000	£2,500

WIND POWER: POINTS TO BEAR IN MIND

The rooftop wind turbine market is in its infancy but manufacturers estimate that once mass production starts systems will be more effective.

In the UK we have 40% of Europe's total wind energy but only 0.5% of our electricity is generated by wind power.

Contact your local Energy Advice Centre for more information on various grant schemes.

HEATING

Most of us currently use gas, oil or electricity to heat our homes but there are a number of alternatives. If you are updating your existing systems, converting a property or building a new one then these are worth exploring.

When it comes to heating your home efficiently – wasting as little fuel and heat as possible – then a full set of heating controls is just as essential as the right kind of boiler. The figures in the charts included in this section are based on the energy use of an average family of four.

 WOOD-FIRED HEATING

Wood is regarded as a sustainable energy source and is promoted as a renewable form of energy. We are being encouraged, through grants, to swap over from coal and oil to wood-burning fuel systems.

OPEN FIRES

In a rural area, burning wood is one of the most environmentally friendly ways of heating individual rooms, or indeed your whole house, because timber is a carbon neutral fuel, i.e., it absorbs as much carbon while growing as it releases when burnt. If you live in an urban area, check with your local council to see if you are allowed to burn wood before you install wood-fired heating or a wood-burning stove.

➡ Remember, open fires need regular maintenance to ensure that they do not present a fire risk.

➡ Timber is usually sourced locally, so transport miles and emissions are minimised.

➡ Heating with wood is not only environmentally friendly, but can also make good economic sense. Timber for fuel is typically up to 30% cheaper than oil or gas.

ALTERNATIVE ECO-FIRE BOXES

Many companies are producing contemporary fires and fireplaces that look authentic without using fossil fuels or wood. There are some ingenious ones available that use denatured ethanol or methylated spirit. A larger burner box can heat a room as big as 376 sq. ft and the smaller burner a room the size of 269 sq. ft.

GREEN BUZZWORDS

Biomass also known as biofuel, comes from organic material.

Domestic biomass applications range from traditional open fires to ultra-modern pellet-burning boilers and heaters.

Non-woody biomass fuels come from sources such as animal waste and high-energy crops (sugar cane, rape and maize).

Woody biomass comes from wood.

WOOD-BURNING STOVES

I believe that wood-burning stoves are the kings of home heating. They are a great alternative to open fires as they are three to four times as efficient at producing heat, are easy to control, and because they have doors it makes them less of a fire risk. Typically wood-burners are made from either cast iron or steel and are available in a wide range of different shapes, sizes and heat outputs.

➡ Cast iron tends to be more ornate or intricate in design, but is less tolerant of overheating or over-firing (a damaging combination of too much fuel and too much air).

➡ Steel is much more tolerant of extreme heat and that tends to translate into a longer lifespan, and modern technology can make it an even more efficient heat conductor.

LOGS

Whether you use open fires or wood burners, your logs need to be well seasoned (ideally for a minimum of two years in a dry store after cutting) and should be free of paint, preservatives or galvanised nails, as these can all emit harmful gases when burnt. Heat logs are an alternative made from sawdust bound together into log shapes, with a flammable substance added for easier lighting.

HOW DOES IT WORK? A stand-alone wood-burning stove provides heat for a single room, with an output range of 5–7kW. It can burn logs or pellets.

 A new eco-friendly wood-burning stove can cost between £400–4,000 installed, plus fuel.

IS MY HOME SUITABLE? You must have a local supplier and relevant storage space for fuel, with air movement around the wood. There must also be an appropriate chimney. Under the Clean Air Act local authorities may declare the whole or part of an area to be a smoke control zone, so if you live in an urban area, check with your local council before you install a wood-burning stove.

ARE GRANTS AVAILABLE? Under the Low Carbon Buildings Programme (LCBP) grants of up to £600 for a wood-pellet-burning stove are available.

HOW MUCH WILL I SAVE? Savings will depend on how much the stove is used and which heat source it is replacing.

ECO-FRIENDLY WOOD BURNERS

The larger the wood-burning stove the more efficient it is.

A wood-burning stove can be installed if you have a house with a working fireplace and a lined chimney.

To find out if you live in a smokeless fuel zone, contact the environmental health department at your local council.

If you do not have a chimney you can install an insulated flu that runs through the house.

WOOD-FIRED CENTRAL HEATING

It is also possible to fuel your central heating by wood, either by installing a back-boiler to certain higher output wood-burners or by considering one of the new technology wood-pellet or chip-burning boilers. Log-fired wood burners with back-boilers are capable of supporting domestic central heating systems in all but the largest of homes and can be very cost effective, but bear in mind that they will need regular attention and you will need a fairly substantial and consistent supply of wood to keep them fed.

FOR THE MORE AMBITIOUS

WOOD-PELLET BOILERS

Wood-pellet or biomass boilers are a recent and increasingly popular development for wood-fired central heating. They range in output from 15kW (the average size needed to heat a three-bedroom semi-detached house) to over 500kW outputs. The pellets themselves are made from the by-products of sawmills and they are carbon neutral. The boilers deliver an efficiency level of around 90% and are normally linked to a heat storage system.

Automatic feeders can be installed to keep wood-pellet boilers running continuously, but they do have a reputation for clogging up and need cleaning regularly. They certainly create far more necessary maintenance.

These boilers tend to be larger than conventional boilers, and must be located where there is easy access for delivery vehicles and unloading. Pellets are available in 20kg and 500kg bags, but are considerably cheaper when bought in bulk. Typical deliveries are 3–5 tonnes (you would need 4–5 tonnes per year to heat a 3-bedroomed home) and require storage in a hopper, silo or bunker to keep them dry. The pellets are transported to the boiler using a feed system, which consists of a flexible auger inside a tube.

A 15kW pellet boiler costs £5,000–14,000 to install and can last over 20 years. Fuel costs are £180–210 per tonne, but you

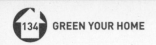

SOLAR WATER HEATING

There are two very different types of solar panel technology. PV systems that generate electricity (see page 121) and solar thermal technology that generates hot water. A solar water-heating system heats the hot water that comes out of your taps and your hot water cylinder (the one in your airing cupboard), instead of using your other means of heating, such as a gas central-heating boiler. When there is not enough solar energy available, your hot water can be supplemented automatically by your central heating boiler. So you will always have hot water throughout the year.

HOW DOES IT WORK? A solar water-heating system has three elements:

- Solar panels or collectors, which can either be flat plate or tube systems.

- Heat transfer system, which uses the accumulated heat to heat water.

- Hot water cylinder, which stores the hot water.

HOW MUCH WILL IT COST? A typical domestic system costs between £3,000 and £5,000 installed. Evacuated tube designs are more expensive than flat plate systems as the technology is more advanced.

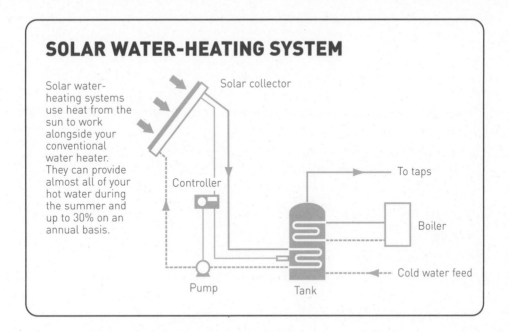

SOLAR WATER-HEATING SYSTEM

Solar water-heating systems use heat from the sun to work alongside your conventional water heater. They can provide almost all of your hot water during the summer and up to 30% on an annual basis.

Solar collector

To taps

Controller

Boiler

Pump

Tank

Cold water feed

IS MY HOUSE SUITABLE? You will need a south-east- to south-west-facing roof measuring 3–4 sq. m, which receives direct sunlight for most of the day. Flat roofs can be used if the panels are installed on an A-frame that is tilted towards the sun. Solar water-heating systems may not be an option if you live in a block of flats, and combination boilers are not compatible as you need to have a hot-water tank for the system to work.

DO I NEED PLANNING PERMISSION? Homeowners are generally able to install microgeneration equipment, such as solar panels, without needing to get planning permission, as long as there is clearly no impact on others. But in some instances, you may need planning consent. This usually applies to listed buildings or homes in a conservation area, but it is always recommended that you check with your local planning authority.

ARE GRANTS AVAILABLE? Up to £400 is available via the Low Carbon Buildings Programme.

HOW MUCH WILL I SAVE? For a three-bedroom home a solar water-heating system could provide up to one third of the hot water requirements, representing a saving of around £50 a year.

HOW LONG WILL IT LAST? Systems usually come with a guarantee of 5–10 years. A detailed check by a professional is recommended every 3–5 years.

£	COST	GRANT	ANNUAL HOT WATER SPEND	% SAVING ON HOT WATER	% SAVING ON ANNUAL ELECTRICITY BILL
	£3,000–£5,000	£400	£150	33.3%	50%

GROUND-, AIR- AND WATER-SOURCE HEAT PUMPS

Ground-source heat pumps (also known as geothermal heat pumps) transfer heat that is stored in the ground (e.g. your garden), into your house to heat your home, and in some cases, to pre-heat domestic hot water. Air-source and water-source heat pumps are also available.

HOW DOES IT WORK? A ground-source heat pump works in the same way as a deep freeze. A mixture of water and antifreeze is pushed through underground pipes. The heat in the ground passes into the extremely cold liquid and it is then pumped back to the heat exchanger, which may be in the garage or an outside room. This heat is extracted and used to heat the home or hot water.

To push the water around the pipes you need to use electricity, but for every unit of electricity used to pump the water, 3–4 units of heat are produced, making it an efficient way of heating a building. What is more, you can use low-tariff electricity, i.e., night time, to do the pumping making quite considerable savings.

IS MY HOUSE SUITABLE? Your garden needs to be big enough to dig a trench or large hole for the ground loop, which is either laid horizontally under a lawn or vertically in bore holes. Although ground-source heat pumps can work with conventional radiators, under-floor heating is preferred because ground-source heat pumps

work best with heating at a lower temperature – standard radiators need to reach higher temperatures than the pumps can provide. If you live near a river, stream or lake then you could have a water- or air-source heat pump that works in the same way.

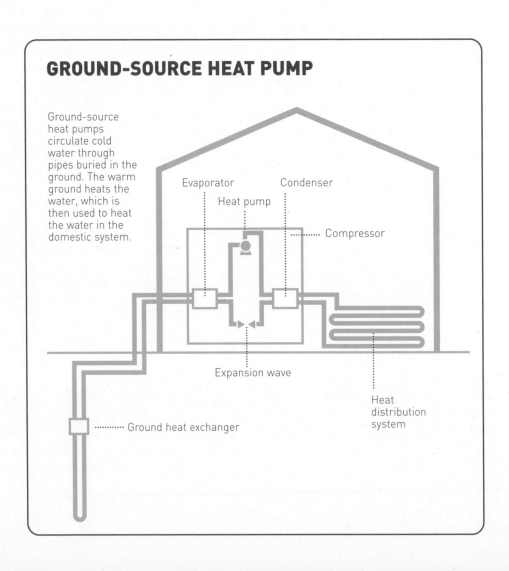

GROUND-SOURCE HEAT PUMP

Ground-source heat pumps circulate cold water through pipes buried in the ground. The warm ground heats the water, which is then used to heat the water in the domestic system.

Evaporator

Condenser

Heat pump

Compressor

Expansion wave

Ground heat exchanger

Heat distribution system

DO I NEED PLANNING PERMISSION No

ARE GRANTS AVAILABLE? A maximum of £1,200 is available from the LCBP. The Scottish Householder Renewables Initiative (SCHRI) provides grants for properties in Scotland.

HOW MUCH WILL I SAVE? Once installed the heating system could save as much as two-thirds of your heating bills – up to £333 a year.

HOW LONG WILL IT LAST? Because the ground-source heat pump is buried underground and contains few mechanical components, it is likely to last at least 20 years.

DOWNSIDE If you want to heat a home quickly, ground-source heating may not be suitable as it doesn't have a great deal of power over a short space of time.

An 8–15 kW ground-source heat pump system can cost between £6,000–12,000.

COST	GRANT	ANNUAL FUEL BILL	% SAVING ON FUEL	£ SAVING HEATING BILL
£6-12,000	£1,500	£1,000	66	333

WATER HEATING APPLIANCES

Don't wait until your existing water heater breaks down; plan now, and decide what you will replace it with when you need to. Do your research now so that you make the right decision when the time comes.

STORAGE TANKS

Generally, water for washing etc., is heated by the same boiler that powers your central heating system. The boiler heats the water that is stored in a tank or cylinder, which is fed either from the mains or a separate cold water tank in the loft. Such systems need to be well insulated. Have a look at yours and check that it is. New models are specially designed to reduce heat loss.

CONDENSING BOILERS

By law, all new boilers must be 'condensing' types which are energy-efficient as they reuse heat from flue gases that traditional boilers allowed to escape out of the chimney.

➡ If you are buying a new boiler it will be rated on a scale of A to G, where band A is the most efficient and band G the least. Only the most efficient boilers also carry the Energy Saving Recommended logo.

➡ Keep your water heater thermostat set at the lowest temperature that provides you with sufficient hot water.

For most households, 50°C (120°F) water is fine (halfway between low and medium setting). Each 18°C (10°F) reduction in water temperature will generally save 3–5% on your water-heating costs. When you are going away on holiday you can turn the thermostat down to the lowest possible setting, or turn the water heater off altogether.

COMBINATION BOILERS

In modern houses, the most usual type of central heating system has a combination boiler. Most combi-boilers, as they are commonly known, run on mains-pressure water, so there is no need to have a tank upstairs or under the roof. Neither do you need a hot water cylinder as they instantly heat the water on demand, and because they run from the mains water supply, you can create an effective power shower without using a pump. Combi-boilers are cheaper to install because there is less plumbing involved than with other types of boiler. However, there is a delay between turning on the tap and getting hot water, when supplied from a tankless heater. The flow rate is limited by how quickly the boiler is able to heat up the water, and you generally can't have two hot water taps running at the same time, which makes them unsuitable for smaller properties.

MEGAFLOW

The megaflow system is a pressurised hot water cylinder that is part way between a traditional heating system and a combination boiler. It is excellent for use in larger houses, but ensure that the size of the hot water cylinder is suitable for your house.

BOILER EFFICIENCY

Boiler efficiency is rated as a percentage, assessing how much of the fuel consumed is converted to heat. This is important because an efficient boiler produces less CO_2; it also consumes less fuel for the same heat output – this will reduce your gas heating costs. If you have to buy a new boiler the purchase price is not as important as the ongoing costs of heating, year after year.

The size of your boiler is dictated by the output you require. This is measured in terms of radiators and hot-water cylinders. Don't make the mistake of buying a considerably oversized boiler. Most boilers installed pre-1989 are as much as 30% oversized. This is an incredible drain on finance as well as energy and these days boiler efficiency calculations are much more advanced.

You'll need to find a Corgi approved engineer to do the work. Corgi, the gas safety watchdog, estimates that there are as many as 20,000 people in the UK working illegally on gas installations.

 Replacing a wall-mounted boiler including draining the system and connecting to the pipe-work could cost in the range of £1,000 upwards

TIPS FOR WATER HEATERS

New boilers are relatively quick to install.

Correct insulation, efficient boilers and tankless water-heating systems all save energy.

Tankless heating costs are much lower than conventional systems.

SEDBUK BOILER EFFICIENCY TABLE

The Seasonal Efficiency of Domestic Boilers in the UK (SEDBUK) rating scheme provides a fair comparison of average boiler efficiency. Only A-rated boilers with efficiencies of over 90% are endorsed by the Energy Saving Trust and carry the Energy Saving Recommended logo.

Band	SEDBUK range
A	90% and above
B	86% - 90%
C	82% - 86%
D	78% - 82%
E	74% - 78%
F	70% - 74%
G	below 70%

WATER

Why do we have to save water?
The infrastructure that delivers us
clean drinking water is only capable
of carrying so much – demand has
exploded, especially in the south of
England, with more people and less
rainfall. Without costing us an
enormous amount of money on new
purification and delivery systems,
we need to reduce our consumption
of water.

USING WATER

Rainfall in the UK is extremely variable: 2006 saw the driest summer on record and 2007 the wettest. There are a number of ways we can minimise our use of water in and around the home, including water metering, rainwater harvesting, other methods of rainwater collection and reusing grey water.

WATER METERS

HOW DO THEY WORK? A water meter records the amount of water being used in your home just like an electricity or gas meter. Your water company checks the meter to work out how much to charge you based on the amount of water you use, rather than being a fixed amount each year calculated on your home's rateable value, which is the traditional way of paying for water.

WHY DO WE NEED THEM? Since 1989 any new supply of water must be fitted with a water meter. If you have an existing supply you can choose to have one fitted and you then have 12 months to change your mind. If you don't change your mind or the supply is taken over by a new owner, the water meter must stay with that supply forever.

The environment often benefits from meters because many people find that they make a conscious effort to use less water when they have a meter fitted. Of course, if you are using less water, you are also heating less water and this could help you save on energy bills and further help to reduce your carbon footprint.

RAINWATER HARVESTING

HOW DOES IT WORK? The system works by transferring all the rainwater that accumulates in your guttering through a filter and deposits it into to a large storage tank. This storage tank can be buried in the ground close to the property to keep the water cool and clean. The tank typically has an electric pump that pumps water back into your home to be used for loos, washing machines and even drinking water. Rainwater is generally safe but you need to make sure that any collected from roofs is lead free: it may have come into contact with lead flashing.

WHAT WILL I NEED?

⮕ If you are going to install a tank in the ground it makes sense to buy the biggest tank you can afford.

⮕ Extras include pumps, filters, overflow siphon and rodent barrier, and mains switching options (for when the water in the tank has run out).

⮕ Labour and labourer's equipment (digger, driver, plumber).

Water companies have to use energy to supply mains water. Water recycling not only saves water but energy too.

IS MY HOUSE SUITABLE? The most common use of stored rainwater is for loos and washing machines, but this means that a typical property needs a separate cold water system for drinking water. This does mean that installing a rainwater-harvesting system in existing properties is expensive. However, if you are renovating a house from scratch and replacing all the plumbing, why not go the extra mile? Tanks don't necessarily have to be buried in the ground. They can also be fitted above ground but in which case will need to be covered or protected in some way to avoid extreme heat, disturbance and evaporation.

DO I NEED PLANNING PERMISSION? No

ARE GRANTS AVAILABLE? No, but the meter will be free (see below).

HOW MUCH WILL I SAVE? Rainwater harvesting saves energy, too, in terms of all the energy costs that the water company incurs when supplying you with water. If you have a meter then you will save approximately £165 per year. The largest most expensive systems can provide around 50% of the annual water requirement for the average home.

Fully installed systems invariably end up being more expensive than quoted for as you need to budget for the extra equipment that goes with the system (see opposite). The larger size tanks plus the fittings will cost between £2,000–3,000 including VAT. The cost of installation will vary, and it will take time to recuperate the initial outlay – probably 5–10 years.

RAINWATER HARVESTING

Rainwater-harvesting systems collect rainwater through guttering and roofing systems and store it underground for use in non-potable purposes, such as watering the garden, washing the car, flushing the loo and running the washing machine.

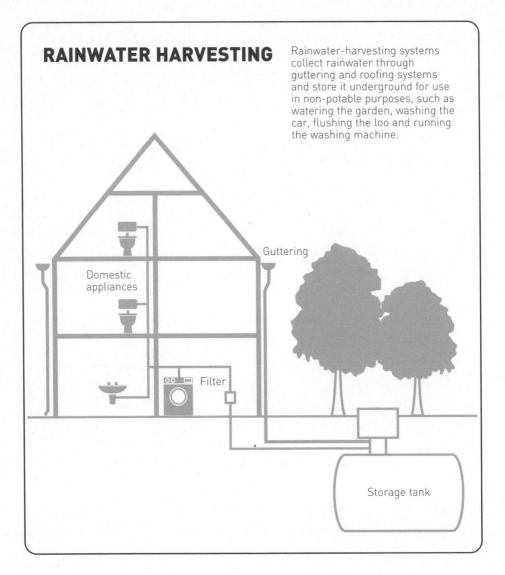

COLLECTING RAINWATER (GARDEN WATER BUTTS)

✔ Use a trap on your downpipe to divert rainwater into the water butt or underground tank or run the downpipe straight into it. The butt should have an overflow to cope with downpours!

✔ It is easier to access the water if the butt sits on a stand, and is fitted with a tap at the base.

✔ If you have only one large water butt, it is worth investing in a submersible pump (cost £50), which will enable you to pump the water through a hosepipe and can even generate enough pressure to allow you to use a spray gun. Otherwise, position several water butts at different points around the house.

 Basic freestanding water butts (200 litre) cost from £30; barrel water butt (235 litre) £65; wall-mounted water butt (100 litre) £90; water column (333 litre) £200.

🚰 GREY WATER

Even if there is not enough rainwater to go around, you don't necessarily have to use treated drinking water to water your plants, which is expensive environmentally and financially.

➤ **GREY WATER** is suitable for re-use and includes water from washing machines, dishwashers, baths, showers and sinks. Make sure that you limit the use of manmade chemicals.

➤ **BLACK WATER** or loo waste is not suitable for re-use or recycling and goes straight into the sewage system or septic tank unless you have a reed-bed system (an ambitious project outside the scope of this book).

You can use some grey water on your garden, but there are a few things to consider first.

☑ Grey water from baths, showers and sinks may contain relatively small amounts of soap and other chemicals, but it is generally considered acceptable for watering garden plants. However, to be on the safe side, do not use it on fruit and vegetable crops.

☑ If you decide to use grey water, it is often possible to divert it to an irrigation system, or to a holding tank. If you store it, don't keep it for too long, or it may stagnate and start to smell.

It is easy to divert grey water if your bathrooms are all on the same waste pipe system and it is above a suitable place for your holding tank.

Price of diversion depends on how much pipe you need – expect to pay £5 for 2m of piping and £10 for a pack of 20 pipe brackets, and holding tank will cost around £2,000.

REUSING GREY WATER

A more sophisticated way of reusing grey water is to install a system that filters and treats all the reclaimed grey water from your house, a bit like a sewage works on a miniature scale. These systems do the following:

- ✔ Collect the waste water.

- ✔ Treat the waste water with a physical filtration process and a biological treatment.

- ✔ Pump it to a storage unit where non-chlorine bleach is used to stop growth of bacteria.

- ✔ Re-use it to flush loos and water gardens; care is needed to ensure that it doesn't mix with mains water.

A system like this is expensive. A typical, off-the-shelf, single house, domestic system can cost approximately £3,000 to purchase, excluding running costs and installation costs. If you are working on a new build or an extensive renovation project, then it would be better value to fit during building work rather than fitting a system at a later date.

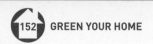

GREY WATER CONSERVATION

Grey water contains nitrogen, phosphorus and potassium, which are beneficial to plants.

It not only saves water and money, but clearly benefits the environment.

Allows you to water your garden without using mains water.

A simple system does not take very long to install, does not cost much and will save you money.

For help with fitting grey water waste pipe systems contact the Sustainable Building Association (for details of website see page 188).

Remember you can always bail out or siphon bathwater and washing up water to water garden plants. Be careful when using strong detergents and soaps.

GREY WATER RECYCLING SYSTEM

These recycling systems
take domestic waste water
(grey water), treat it and
store it for use in the garden
and for flushing loos.

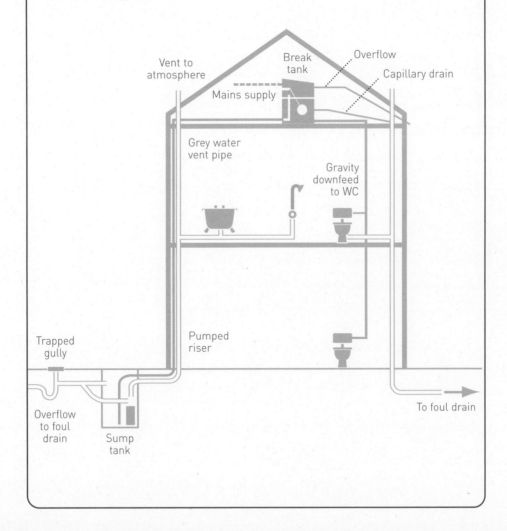

Vent to
atmosphere

Break
tank

Overflow

Capillary drain

Mains supply

Grey water
vent pipe

Gravity
downfeed
to WC

Trapped
gully

Pumped
riser

Overflow
to foul
drain

Sump
tank

To foul drain

The Green Outdoors

BE ECO-FRIENDLY OUTDOORS

If you are looking to green your home, then a good place to start is your outdoor space, whether it be small back yard or a large garden. There are a number of ways of becoming eco-friendly outdoors, including using natural resources in a sustainable way and encouraging a wide range of plants and wildlife. At the same time you can create a relaxing green space. By working with nature and not against it and following organic ideals, it can even make gardening less hard work. Take green literally and get some plants back into your life.

GREENER GARDENS

Gardening sounds like a green activity but it can have a negative impact on the environment. The greenest solution would probably be to let the weeds grow wild, but this is not always a realistic one – especially if you want to create a useable family space. Fortunately, if you are concerned, it is possible to look after your garden and help the environment at the same time.

CREATING A WILDLIFE GARDEN

Today many people are opting for low-maintenance gardens, but clearing a garden of trees and hedges can disturb wildlife habitats. The trend for such gardens, as well as modern gardening techniques – including the use of pesticides, herbicides and miracle feeds – has resulted in a reduction in wildlife in urban areas. However, you don't have to do very much to attract wildlife to your garden. You do not need a jungle; look at your existing plants and assess their suitability. Choose new plants carefully, considering their potential to provide pollen, nectar, fruit or seed valuable for wildlife . Avoid using harmful chemicals in the garden, and make sure that you create suitable habitats – the wildlife will come of its own accord. Once you have attracted insects and other small invertebrates, such as worms, larger species (frogs, birds, hedgehogs and squirrels) will follow as they hunt for food. (For advice see Greener Gardens websites on page 189).

RECYCLING

A huge variety of recycled materials can be used for jobs in the garden – from old, broken-up paving slabs to build patios and rockeries, to used coffee grounds to keep slugs away from your lettuces. You can buy plant containers from secondhand shops and all manner of gardening items from architectural salvage

TOP TIPS FOR WILDLIFE GARDENS

Ponds create perfect habitats for wildlife. Even a large plastic bowl sunk in the ground or a bath for the birds will help.

Try making your own bird table from leftover wood. Make sure it is tall, ideally with a roof (hanging feeders are excellent too), and site it so that squirrels and cats can't get to it.

Avoid using chemical fertilisers and pesticides – use good compost to feed your soil.

If you don't have much space you can plant climbing ivy that gives cover for birds and insects.

Create a wild corner where you don't do too much weeding. Add some old wood or rocks under which small animals can burrow and plant native wildflowers to attract insects.

Invest in a wildlife reference book – your garden may be a haven for something rare and, if so, it could be protected.

companies. In addition, you can reuse certain household goods in the garden – for instance yoghurt pots are ideal for growing seeds, but even old sinks can be adapted as bird baths or planters.

COMPOSTING

Ideally, every home with a garden should have a compost heap. If organic waste from your kitchen has to be transported to a landfill site, it uses fuel to get there. And, once there, if it is not carefully managed, it also produces methane, a notorious greenhouse gas.

Like recycling, composting will make a difference to the amount of rubbish you produce in a week; you will also produce compost you can use on your garden. It will not take up much of your time and will become second nature very quickly. Less rubbish in landfill is good for the environment. Many councils offer subsidised composting bins so the cost is low; check in your area for details of schemes in operation.

INCLUDE any organic matter but a mixture of kitchen and garden waste is ideal. It can include shredded paper, cardboard and cotton. Grass clippings are fine (they are an activator and help to get the compost going), provided they are mixed with other drier ingredients so they don't turn to slime. Urine is also very good at speeding up the decomposition process.

AVOID cooked foods, because they attract rats, and also avoid pernicious weeds such as ground elder, bindweed and couch grass, because they can survive the composting process.

SITE your compost heap well away from your garden door – it can smell.

MORE TIPS FOR GREENER GARDENS

PEAT is non-renewable but it is still being widely used by gardeners, and vast peat bogs throughout Europe are being destroyed to satisfy the demand. Make sure any compost you buy is peat-free and try to buy plants grown in peat alternatives — they are readily available.

JUST PRODUCING and distributing 1kg of chemical fertiliser generates 6kg of carbon dioxide. Try to use compost, manure and liquid seaweed instead of inorganic fertiliser.

THE AVERAGE LAWNMOWER produces more than 1kg of carbon dioxide emissions every week (petrol lawnmowers produce more CO_2 than electric versions), whereas 2 sq. m of uncut grass produces enough oxygen to supply an adult for a year. If you have enough space, let some parts of the lawn grow wild and mix wild flowers in with the grass. Where you have to cut the grass, you would ideally use a manual lawnmower.

GROWING YOUR OWN FOOD is an obvious way to reduce carbon emissions. Even if you don't have an allotment, try growing your own vegetables in your garden, window boxes or pots inside.

FENCING AND HEDGING

As in other areas of the garden try to make your choice of boundary as green as possible. Regular applications of preservative or paint (with no or low VOCs) will maintain an exisiting timber fence so that it will look good indefinitely. Take into consideration the growing requirements of your hedges, as well as clipping and pruning them to keep them healthy.

FENCING

While you may be considering eco-friendly fencing options, if you live in a conservation or other designated area, or in a listed building, your choice of fence and/or hedge may be affected by legislation and you will need to bear this is mind, too.

CHOOSING MATERIALS

Brick walls make good permanent boundaries but not only are they expensive to build, they are also costly for the planet. They are made from an unsustainable material and require a great deal of energy, both in terms of quarrying and in firing. Reclaimed bricks provide a greener option.

If you are using new wood ensure that it has a FSC (PEFC) certificate (see pages 20–1), so that it is sourced from a well managed forest.

There are plenty of alternatives to hardwood fencing, and many of them are not only greener but cheaper too. Softwood treated with an eco-friendly preservative is fine for most wooden fencing, and you can stain it or paint it any colour you like. However, do not use toxic wood preservatives such as creosote.

TRADITIONAL FENCING

Traditional fencing made from coppiced woodland is 100% sustainable. Depending on species, an area of woodland can be ready to supply its next crop in anything between 5–30 years. By buying local products you cut transportation costs and support local craftspeople. In addition, well-managed coppice woodlands provide a wide range of habitats and benefit local wildlife. If you live in a rural or well-wooded area, you may want to consider different types of traditional fencing, including the following.

- Continuous fencing is woven from wooden rods, known as hurdles. Generally, these are used in the short term (3–5 years) while planting or hedging grows.

- Hurdle panels are similar to the above but in a timber frame.

- Post-and-rail fencing is an inexpensive way of creating a boundary. It can be sawn in oak, when no treatment is necessary, or a softwood, which requires preservative, or for a more rustic look in cleft oak or chestnut.

TYPE	SIZE	COST
Willow hurdle	180 x 180 cm (6 x 6 ft)	£38
Hazel hurdle	180 x 180 cm (6 x 6 ft)	£45
Willow screen	180 x 180 cm (6 x 6 ft)	£55
Bamboo screen	200 x 200 cm (6½ x 6½ ft)	£59

ALTERNATIVE FENCING

Today composite fencing, made from recycled materials, such as plastic, used pallets, sawdust and cardboard, is available. Manufacturers claim that it is an environmentally friendly alternative to timber; requires less maintenance because of its resistance to water, insects and rotting; and needs no painting or staining. Some companies offer 25-year guarantees on this type of fencing. When it does need replacing, it can be recycled once again.

 A 240 x 180 cm composite fencing panel is around £95. A 240 x 90 cm panel is around £65.

HEDGING

Consider native species, such as oak, hazel, hawthorn, beech and hornbeam, which form the most suitable habitat for our native wildlife. When choosing what type of hedge to plant, bear in mind your location and climate – The Royal Horticultural Society website (www.rhs.org.uk) offers advice.

Remember that the fastest growing hedge plants, like the infamous Leylandii, do not necessarily stop growing at the height you want them! The advantages of hedges include the following:

➡ **FOOD AND SHELTER FOR BIRDS AND INSECTS** A hawthorn hedge with red haws in autumn, or the berries on a spotted laurel, pyracantha or holly provide sustenance for birds. And insects love lavender, oleaster and hawthorn, too. As well as feeding the wildlife, hedges give shelter. Always check that fledglings have left their nest before clipping your hedge. The occupied nests of all wild birds are protected by law.

NOISE POLLUTION Dense evergreen hedges are a useful way of reducing noise levels (although they won't eliminate them altogether). The degree of sound deadening is influenced by the height, maturity and density of a hedge. In addition, hedges planted for sound proofing are also known to absorb air pollution, which is particularly useful near herb and vegetable gardens and children's play areas.

An average 10m hedge with 3 per metre costing £7 each works out at £210.

A wall of the same length and height would cost approx £10,000, assuming a builder does it for you.

A fence would be a less expensive, perhaps about £400.

PATIOS, PAVING AND DRIVEWAYS

Most gardens need at least one hard surface, whether it is a patio, driveway or off-street parking. Clearly, all the stone, aggregates and other products needed for jobs such as these do have considerable impact on the environment. However, FSC-certified wood for decking is a green choice.

STONE

Avoid stones such as marble and granite that are mined from deep in the ground and therefore require energy-intensive, high-polluting extraction processes. Choose softer types of stone such as sandstone and slate. These are found closer to the earth's surface and are much easier to mine, requiring less energy. But remember there is a finite amount of stone available and that it is possible to source reclaimed stone flags, setts and cobbles. If you buy imported stone, ask whether your supplier has inspected the quarries they buy from to check that they are well-managed.

BARK CHIPS

Bark chips are inexpensive, easily available and easy to lay. It is an ideal material for childrens' play areas but will need regular topping-up. You can buy FSC-approved products at garden centres.

GRAVEL

Inexpensive and low maintenance. Less green than bark chips but good for paths and drives. Buy just one bag to start with and see what you think before you lay more.

PERMEABLE CONCRETE

Permeable paving slabs have been introduced in the last few years as a solution to the problem of storm water run-off, depletion of underground water-bearing rock and over-burdened sewers. These materials are relatively new and not widely available (and are, therefore, expensive), but they are sure to become more popular.

CLAY BRICKS

Bricks are attractive and can be laid in a variety of patterns, including herringbone, but are more expensive than ordinary concrete blocks. They also use a lot of energy in production. (See also pages 22–3.)

MATERIAL	COST
Stone	£26-36 per sq. m.
Bark chips	£15 per bag
Gravel	£3.99 per bag
Permeable concrete	around £40 per sq. m.
Clay bricks	45p each

OFF-ROAD PARKING

More and more home owners are converting parts of their front gardens to paving slabs or tarmac driveways which gives them off-road parking and low maintenance outside space. Hard surfaces can increase surface water run-off by up to 50%, resulting in an increased volume of water entering the drainage systems, which increases the risk of flooding.

PLANNING AND PREPARING YOUR AREA

Setting out the area to be paved and preparing the ground is a large part of the job: clearing it of vegetation, levelling it and making sure there is adequate drainage. All paving should be designed to drain freely to gullies or other disposal points. A recommended slope is usually quoted as 1 in 40. In practice, 1 in 80 is adequate for smaller, domestic areas. Whenever possible, paving should be laid so that rainwater flows into borders or ponds, rather than down the drain or onto the road. Pave as small an area as possible.

MATERIALS TO AVOID

TARMAC BITUMINOUS MACADAM (to give it its proper name) is made by coating aggregates with bitumen, a sticky mixture of hydrocarbons produced as part of the crude oil distillation process. Laid hot and rolled smooth, it is suitable for roads, drives and forecourts, but not for use in gardens, where it is vulnerable to attack by moss. It is relatively cheap, and usually black in colour.

CONCRETE SLABS The most commonly used paving product over the last 10–15 years. Mass production has driven down the cost, and there is a huge range of colours and shapes. Low maintenance but must be laid correctly.

AND REMEMBER British stone such as York stone from the Pennines is expensive and becoming scarce. Try not to use non-renewable products.

DECKING

When laying timber decking it is important to choose your materials carefully. Always use timber from sustainable forest sources (FSC certified) and remember the following.

➡ If the foundations are not properly prepared, your decking will warp and twist when winter comes, and the only solution will be to take it up and start again.

➡ Decking should have a membrane underneath it to stop weeds from growing through the cracks – avoid concreting.

▶ A slope of around 1:100 should be built into a deck to help the surface drain and prevent standing water. Grooved deck boards are designed to aid water drainage and should be laid in the direction of the fall, away from any adjoining buildings.

▶ Use corrosion-resistant screws for fixing. The advantages of screws over nails are that they are more secure and they enable boards to be lifted easily to gain access below the deck for maintenance and repairs.

CHOOSING TIMBER

▶ Pressure-treated softwoods are the most popular decking material because of their availability, ease of working and cost effectiveness. Hardwoods such as cedar are more expensive than softwoods, but last longer and are more resistant to rot.

▶ Grooved deck boards are often marketed as 'anti-slip' but there is no evidence that they perform any better than plain decking: the key factor in preventing slippery boards is to keep the deck surface clean and free from mildew, algae and moss.

▶ Reclaimed timber is an option. Sources include: scaffolding planks, wood from boatyards and river landing stages, and old railway sleepers (although these tend to bleed tar).

TIMBER ALTERNATIVE

As with fencing, composite decking made from various recycled materials is an option worth considering. It can be worked like wood – cut or sawn and sanded – but it won't rot, warp or splinter. No stains or sealants are needed, just minimal maintenance.

FURNITURE AND GARDEN ACCESSORIES

When it is time to sit back and enjoy the fruits of your labour, you will need furniture that is not only comfortable and stylish, but also able to withstand the British climate.

CHOOSING MATERIALS

- **RECYCLED PLASTIC** is a low maintenance, environmentally friendly and economical alternative to timber. It has the appearance of wood with the advantages of plastic. There are many colour ranges available and the only maintenance required is a wipe over with a damp cloth and detergent.

- **WOOD** If you have a bigger budget, furniture made from natural wood is lovely, but remember to check that it comes from a sustainable source with an FSC certificate. Try avoid imported hardwoods, particularly mahogany – opt for recycled ones if you do.

- **REFURBISHING** Your existing hardwood garden furniture can be refurbished with one application of a water-based finish treatment applied by brush straight from the can. This will bring greying or heavily stained wood back to its original natural lustre.

- **HAMMOCKS** are perfect for relaxing in the garden and they are made from environmentally friendly materials, including rope, bamboo and cotton.

Buying secondhand garden furniture and decorative items is a great way to find green alternatives for your garden, such as dining tables and chairs, statues, urns, sundials, benches and fountains. Start looking in auctions or at architectural salvage centres. You can find items in a wide range of materials including stone, wood and wrought iron.

RESTORING ANTIQUE GARDEN FURNITURE

> **IRON** Iron furniture needs to be carefully maintained. It should be washed, sealed and checked for deterioration.

> **WOOD** Teak oil can help restore the appearance of old furniture and maintain the colour and appearance of new furniture. It protects and enhances the wood by replacing the natural oils lost through weathering. Clean the wood with warm water (with a mild detergent mixed into it) and then use a soft damp cloth to wipe off and remove any dust or grit. After you have done this, you now need to leave the wood to dry naturally before you apply the oil.

GARDEN LIGHTING

Garden lighting can waste a lot of electricity because the bulbs are too far away from the features they're supposed to be lighting, and most of the light disappears into thin air. Switch to energy efficient bulbs and direct your garden lights to reflect off walls, furniture, plants and water features. Don't forget to turn them off when you come indoors! You can also buy solar powered lights to place at key points in the garden. They use no mains electricity so don't generate any carbon dioxide.

 LAWNS

Like all plants, grass consumes carbon dioxide and releases oxygen. So you can enjoy your green space and help the environment at the same time. You can create a lawn using seed or turf. Both methods have advantages.

CHOOSING MATERIALS

➡ Turf is quick to lay, and can be laid at almost any time of year, as long as the weather is good. However, it must be laid almost as soon as it is delivered, and you must keep it watered if you lay it in summer.

➡ Seed is a more environmentally sensible choice – it is less expensive and you can choose the grasses that make up the seed mixture to suit your conditions, which is important if you have a shady or wet area. Different types and qualities of seed are available for different situations, and seed will keep until weather conditions are exactly right for sowing. The grass will take some time to grow so it is not for the impatient or instant gardener. You must keep off the grass while it is growing.

£	TYPE OF LAWN	COST PER SQM	LABOUR COST
	Seed	£1.50	£200
	Turf	£3.50	£200

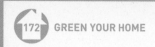

LAYING A LAWN WITH TURF

An average lawn in a town garden will take two people 2–4 days to create. The amount of work depends on its size and the condition of the ground. Much of the time will be spent preparing the site, so the labour (unless you are doing it yourself) is likely to cost considerably more than the materials.

LAWNMOWERS Manual lawn movers are quieter than petrol or electric mowers and will also keep you fit! They are also less expensive and more eco-friendly.

Cylinder manual mower with 20l box	£40
Larger manual mower with 35l box	£70

CARING FOR YOUR LAWN

A week after laying new turf, mow the lawn, but cut off no more than 2.5cm (1in).

Water in the evening – you will lose less water through evaporation.

If there's no rain, water using harvested rainwater or grey water.

WATERING THE GARDEN

Whatever the weather, it is always sensible to plan for future water shortages and hosepipe bans. At the same time, minimising run-off from paved areas is essential to reduce the risk of flooding.

INSTALLING AN AUTOMATIC WATERING SYSTEM

Watering systems for large gardens can be expensive but it is not difficult to install a basic system of plastic pipes to take the strain out of watering a small, urban garden.

SIX REASONS TO HAVE A WATERING SYSTEM

- Energy can be used at night when there is less demand.
- You can keep all plants alive rather than having to replace them.
- Reduces the soil erosion.
- Suitable for all types of garden.
- Suits all soil types.
- You can use rainwater directly from water butts.

TOP TIPS TO REDUCE WATERING REQUIREMENTS

Mulch any areas of bare soil with well-rotted compost or manure, or bark or wood chippings. Mulches will conserve moisture in the soil and help keep the weeds at bay.

Choose the correct plants for your soil. If your soil tends to dry out, grow plants that are relatively drought tolerant, such as herbs, prairie grasses, and many Mediterranean plants.

Water plants in the evening when the heat has gone – you will lose less water through evaporation.

Put in permanent 'seep' hoses. These are perforated hoses that are laid in borders and beds and deliver water slowly direct to the soil surface.

Grow ground-cover plants. These provide leaf cover, which helps to retain the moisture in the soil.

If you install an irrigation system, use a water timer on your tap and set it to water your garden in the evening.

DIY DRIP FEED SYSTEM

The first thing to check is the pressure of your garden tap using a simple pressure gauge. To water 4 sq. m of flowerbeds you will need pressure of at least 40–80 psi (pounds per sq. in); for a drip-by-drip system 10–20 psi will be sufficient.

YOU WILL NEED

> **TAP** Connect the system to your garden tap either directly or via a timer. It is a good idea to use a splitter, so that you can use the tap to fill a watering can without having to disconnect the irrigation system.

> **FILTER** Make sure the water goes through a filter to trap lime scale and impurities which might otherwise block the system.

> **PIPELINE** Measure the total length of your run and use main supply hose to distribute water around the garden. You can design the system to go around corners and avoid obstacles using a combination of connectors (elbows, tees, and crosses). Remember to buy an end stop for the main pipe.

> **DELIVERY SYSTEM** Use tube adaptors to connect the main hose to narrower pipes which run into the areas you want to water, and attach drippers, sprinklers, or sprays wherever you need them. You will need a special hole punch, a sharp knife and a bowl of hot water to soften the plastic – it makes it easier to insert rigid components such as dripper nozzles.

Kits are available: £45 for a starter kit for small gardens; £100 if you have digital timers and more outlets.

ROOFS

Whether you are renovating your existing roof or need a completely new roof, bear in mind 'reduce, reuse and recycle', and consider all the options that are available. Maintenance of existing roofs is key to being green and will prevent damage to your property caused by bad weather. Although there are different types of conventional roofing materials – including clay, slate and concrete tiles – there are also more eco-friendly alternatives such as biomass roofing (thatch and wooden tiles) and the ultimate roofing alternative – a green roof – which uses a layer of vegetation on top of the main roof covering.

ROOFING MATERIALS

Choice of roofing material depends largely on the roof's shape, style and the local area. One of the greenest solutions is to choose reclaimed or recycled materials – including tiles, slates, ridges, chimneys, chimney pots and finials – to match the existing roof.

CONVENTIONAL MATERIALS

▶ **CLAY TILES** Clay tiles have been used for centuries and are very durable (they were used as a fireproof alternative to wooden shingles, see below). However, extracting clay from the ground has an adverse environmental impact and its sustainability is at risk. Clay tile production requires a great deal of energy, both in terms of quarrying and the power used in firing. Consequently, it's worth looking after such a roof and reusing tiles where possible, or sourcing reclaimed clay tiles.

▶ **SLATES** A highly durable and relatively maintenance-free roof covering, slate comes from natural (quarried) stone that is split into thin sheets. The cost to the environment is great as slate has to be quarried and transported – often from China, Brazil, Spain and India. Reclaimed and recycled slate tiles (made up of 60% slate) are available, which are more eco-friendly options.

▶ **CONCRETE TILES** Although they are usually a cheaper option, it's best to avoid using concrete tiles as they are far from being either biodegradable or environmentally friendly. Do not be tempted to use concrete tiles in place of slates: the original timbers may not be strong enough to support them.

BIOMASS ROOFING

One of the oldest forms of roofing has recently seen a revival of interest and employs natural plant materials (straw, reeds, wood). These are only truly sustainable if they are produced in an eco-friendly way – grown, harvested and made locally from renewable sources.

➤ **THATCH** Thatching is popular, not only because of its charm and character but also because it is sustainable. Generally, thatch is made from water reed, wheat reed (a type of straw cut with a binder) and long straw. Life spans vary: water reed lasts about 50–60 years; wheat reed about 25–40 years and long straw 10–20 years. A thatched roof is worth restoring, because if it is replaced by other heavier roofing materials the roofing timbers may need to be strengthened.

Thatch roofs do not catch fire any more frequently than roofs covered with 'hard' materials, but are difficult to extinguish once a fire takes hold. It is imperative that precautions are taken to reduce the risk. Being an organic material, thatch is susceptible to decay and decomposition and animals and birds can also cause damage.

➤ **WOOD** Wooden tiles, also called shingles, have been used in Britain since medieval times, but were superseded by fire-resistant materials such as clay or slate tiles. However, they are once again being used, this time as a sustainable material. Today there are two main types of wooden tiles, which are made for new roofs and refurbishment work: sawn shingles and split shakes. Shingles are thinner and smoother than shakes, which have a more rustic look. Shingled roofs can last more than 60 years depending on the wood. Wooden roofs need to be kept free of moss and lichen as they can cause the wood to rot.

GREEN ROOFS

Buildings can be green, quite literally, if you give them a green roof as an alternative to traditional materials (see pages 177–8). You can buy stonecrop (*Sedum acre*) in rolls similar to lawn turf and it can survive in a bed of soil just 5 cm (2 in) deep. It's like a living carpet for outdoor use. It can also live without water for up to 28 days. If the roof will take deeper planting beds, you can grow other plants as well. Green roofs are better suited for flat roofs.

WHAT IS A GREEN ROOF?

A green roof is a layer of plants that sits on top of the main roof covering of a building. There are two main types of green roof. 'Intensive' roofs comprise relatively deep soil layers, and can support a wide variety of plants, and as a consequence they need a high degree of maintenance, like a conventional garden. They are also heavy and may require an existing roof to be reinforced. 'Extensive' roofs on the other hand comprise shallow, lightweight layers of low-growing, free-draining, low-maintenance vegetation that is capable of withstanding extremes of weather. Extensive green roofs require little or no additional structural support.

WHAT ARE THE BENEFITS?

➤ **INSULATION** Green roofs are probably the ultimate form of insulation: they keep the building below cooler in the summer and reduce heat loss in the winter, saving energy.

➤ **DURABILITY** Green roofs can extend the life of a flat roof membrane by 50 years by acting as insulator, sponge, and cushion when walked on.

➤ **REDUCTION IN POLLUTANTS** When the black tar base of asphalt and flat roof materials is heated it sends harmful pollutants into the atmosphere. Green roofs are pollution free.

➤ **OXYGEN PRODUCTION** Plants not only convert carbon dioxide into oxygen through photosynthesis, but they also help remove pollutants from the atmosphere.

➤ **RAINWATER** Green roofs absorb a large percentage of rainwater and this reduces run-off lowering the risk of flooding.

WHAT TYPES OF BUILDINGS ARE SUITABLE?

Green roof schemes particularly suit blocks of flats and mansion blocks that already have flat roofs. Talk to your management company or resident's committee about looking into the costs.

BEFORE YOU BEGIN

☑ Prior to designing and constructing your rooftop garden, you must first determine if your roof can support the additional weight of soil and plants. It will need to comply with building regulations as it affects the structure, and a structural engineer will need to calculate whether the roof can deal with the extra weight.

☑ The structural capacity will largely dictate the type of rooftop garden that you can build. Roofs with limited structural capacity may be unsuitable for a whole green roof.

☑ Access to your roof is important. You will need to transport construction and maintenance materials and may need to consider the need for electricity. Typical access includes stairs or fire escapes which need to comply with building regulations.

☑ For rooftop gardens, you may be able to bear steel or concrete cross beams on the outer walls to enable more weight to be added to the roof.

WHAT IS INVOLVED?

Using every inch of roof space for planting is a way to make substantial savings on energy costs because it protects and extends the life of the roof membrane. What makes this approach to roof maintenance (and gardening) pay, is the protection offered by layering matting, soil and plant material on top of the roof membrane. The lightweight plastic matting provides an air pocket between the membrane and the soil, allowing excess rainwater to pass through to drains, and it blocks roots so they cannot damage the membrane. Lightweight soil 8–30cm deep is placed on top of the matting, and the weight of the soil is well below the most conservative weight load limits of most roofs.

PLANTING AND MAINTENANCE

Low-maintenance roof gardens made up of alpine plants require little or no care. Alpine plants have adapted to poor rocky mountainous soils. They can stand drought conditions and they will survive and thrive with minimal care. However, if you are interested in a more ornamental (higher-maintenance) garden, this can be created with the use of drip irrigation systems (developed in Israel where water is at a premium) that will supplement rainfall and minimise water use.

PITCHED GREEN ROOFS

The benefits of green roofs are becoming increasingly understood by those in the UK construction industry. Waterproofing systems for pitched green roofs tend to be simpler than those for flat green roofs, as the pooling of water is less of a problem. Nevertheless, as with all waterproofing products, the success of the system is dependent upon the quality of installation.

 Installation of a basic green roof garden using low maintenance alpine plants is £100–200 per sq. m. Maintenance consisting of removal of weeds and dead leaves once or twice a year should cost no more than £200 per year. Checking the drip systems and other electronics is dependent on the hourly rate of your maintenance worker.

ADVANTAGES OF GREEN ROOFS

It exchanges carbon dioxide with oxygen, like a tree.

No longer just for eco-warriors – now they are more accessible for anyone living in an urban or rural environment.

Create more green open spaces and provide habitats for birds and insects.

STRUCTURE OF A GREEN ROOF

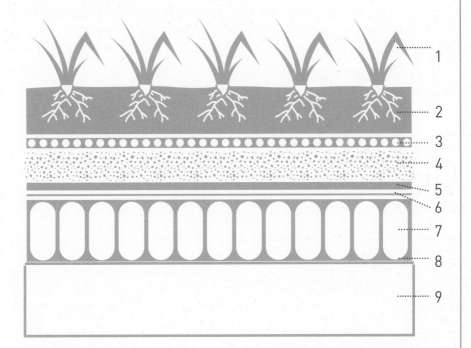

1 Vegetation
2 Growing Medium
3 Filter Membrane
4 Drainage layer
5 Waterproof/root repellant layer
6 Support panel
7 Thermal Insulation
8 Vapour control layer
9 Structural support

Green roofs are made up of several layers of different materials, which support, insulate and protect the roof below. They also offset the lack of oxygen produced by paved and minimalist urban gardens.

GLOSSARY

Aggregate
Sand and stone particles of different sizes that combine with a binder to create the structural strength of concrete, cob, mortars, and plasters.

Black water
Water that contains potential toxins (such as synthetic chemicals or human faeces) as it leaves a building through a drain.

Caulking
The application of flexible sealing compounds to close up gaps in buildings.

Carbon emissions
The amount of carbon dioxide, the main greenhouse gas that is contributing to climate change, released into the atmosphere.

Carbon footprint
Your carbon footprint is the amount of CO_2 that enters the atmosphere because of the electricity and fuel you use and the products you buy. It's measured in tonnes of CO_2.

Cellulose
The primary constituent of the cell walls of most plants; in building, the term usually refers to recycled newspaper insulation, though straw and wood are both also forms of cellulose.

Cement plaster
Mix containing Portland cement, hydrated lime, and sand; often called stucco.

Clay
Soil component that is water absorbent, becomes plastic and sticks to itself when wet, and hardens when dried; originates from feldspathic rock, such as granite.

Climate change
Any long-term significant change in the average weather (temperature, rainfall, wind patterns) that a given region experiences.

Compact fluorescent lamp (CFL)
A type of fluorescent lamp also known as a compact fluorescent light bulb or energy saving light bulb.

Convection
The transfer of heat by physically moving molecules from one place to another.

Drainage box
Outer edge of a living roof that holds materials in place but allows water to escape.

Fossil fuels
Fuel sources formed from the fossilised remains of dead plants and animals found near the surface of the Earth's crust.

Glazing
Glass used in doors and windows.

Global warming
The increase in the average measured temperature of the Earth's near-surface air and oceans since the mid-20th century, and its projected continuation.

Greenhouse gases
Gases in the atmosphere that insulate the Earth's surface from extremes of temperature. The main greenhouse gases are water vapour, carbon dioxide, methane, ozone and nitrous oxide.

Grey water
Water that contains no potential toxins, (such as synthetic chemicals or human faeces) as it leaves a building through a drain.

Insulated glass
Glass unit made up of at least two panes separated by a sealed space filled with air or other gases.

Insulation
Material used to resist the movement of heat.

Light emitting diodes (LEDs)
One of the major display technologies used in electronics equipment. High power versions that are now available mean they can now be used to provide low-energy lighting.

Light pipes
Pipes used in building for transporting or distributing natural or artificial light.

Lime plaster
Mix containing lime putty, sand, and sometimes a fibre such as chopped straw.

Lime wash
Watered-down lime putty sometimes with colour added, used as a sealer for earth- and lime-plastered surfaces.

Living roof
Multi-layered roof skin consisting of a waterproof membrane, insulation, drainage layer, growing medium, and plants; also known as a green roof.

Low-emissivity (Low-E) coatings
Microscopically thin, virtually invisible, metal or metallic oxide layers deposited on a window or skylight glazing surface primarily to reduce how fast heat flows through a structure by suppressing radiative heat flow.

MDF (Medium Density Fibreboard)
An engineered wood product formed by breaking down softwood into wood fibres, binding them together with wax and resin, and forming panels by applying high temperature and pressure.

Microgeneration
The production of small-scale energy using sustainable sources by individuals, businesses and communities to meet their own needs.

Mortar
Any of a variety of mixes that bind stacked units in a structure.

Petrochemicals
Chemical products made from raw materials of petroleum or other hydrocarbon origin.

Photovoltaics
The direct production of electrical current from solar radiant energy.

Plaster
Mixture of a fine aggregate, a binder and water to create a seamless building skin applied wet that dries to a hard, protective coating.

Pointing
The process of cleaning, filling gaps in, and compressing fresh, partially cured mortar.

Portland cement
Mineral binder used in concrete and plaster mixes; made by burning limestone, clays, shales, or other ingredients containing alumina and silica.

Radiation
The transfer of heat through space by means of electromagnetic energy.

Rainwater harvesting
A system that involves capturing rainwater and storing it for later use.

Renewable energy
Energy generated from natural resources – such as sunlight, wind, rain, tides and geothermal heat – which are renewable (naturally replenished).

Smart meter
An advanced meter that identifies energy consumption in more detail than a conventional meter; the most sophisticated smart meters communicate information back to the local energy supplier for monitoring and billing.

Under-floor heating
Heating system in which a heated substance is passed . through tubing embedded in or under flooring material.

Volatile Organic Compounds (VOCs)
Organic chemical compounds that have high enough vapour pressures under normal conditions to significantly vaporise and enter the atmosphere.

Weatherstripping
Weatherstripping is the process of sealing openings such as doors and windows from the elements.

Wind power
Electricity created by wind spinning a turbine that in turn spins the rotor of a generator.

DIRECTORY

ENVIRONMENTAL ORGANISATIONS

Centre for Alternative Technology (CAT)
CAT is concerned with the search for globally sustainable, whole and ecologically sound technologies and ways of life.
Tel. 01654 705950
www.cat.org.uk

Environmental Law Foundation (ELF)
National UK charity that helps people use the law to protect and improve their local environment and quality of life. Specialist lawyers and consultants provide free guidance and support to those in need of assistance.
Tel. 020 7404 1030
www.elflaw.org

Friends of the Earth
(England, Wales and Northern Ireland)
Environmental charity.
Tel. 020 7490 1555
www.foe.co.uk

Friends of the Earth Scotland
Tel. 0131 243 2700
www.foe-scotland.org.uk
www.green-office.org.uk

Forest Stewardship Council (FSC)
International organisation promoting sustainable forest management.
Tel. 01686 413 916
www.fsc.org

Greenpeace
Environmental charity.
Tel. 020 7865 8100
www.greenpeace.org.uk

Natural England
Aims to conserve and enhance the natural environment for its intrinsic value, the wellbeing and enjoyment of people and the economic prosperity that it brings.
Tel. 0845 600 3078
www.naturalengland.org.uk
www.natureonthemap.org.uk

Soil Association
Runs an FSC-approved woodland management programme and supports organic farming.
Tel. 0117 929 0661 or 01453 752985
www.soilassociation.org

WWF (World Wide Fund for Nature)
International organisation supporting nature and the environment
Tel. 01483 426444
www.wwf.org.uk

LOCAL AND NATIONAL GOVERNMENTAL WEBSITES

Environment Agency
A public body for protecting and improving the environment in England and Wales.
Tel. 0870 850 6506
www.environment-agency.gov.uk

Find and contact your local MP
www.direct.gov.uk

UKPlanning
Planning advice. Find out about any future plans which might be damaging to your local environment.
www.ukplanning.com

Department for Environment, Food and Rural Affairs (DEFRA)

The UK government, the Scottish Executive, the Welsh Assembly Government and the Northern Ireland Administration have agreed upon a set of principles that provide a basis for sustainable development policy in the UK.
www.defra.gov.uk

ENERGY AND ELECTRICITY

The Sustainable Building Association (AECB)

Promotes green building and provides the tools and knowledge to create low-energy buildings.
www.aecb.net
www.carbonlite.org.uk

British Wind Energy Association (BWEA)

Promotes and monitors wind energy.
Tel. 020 7901 3000
www.bwea.com

Carbon Trust

Aims to accelerate the move to a low carbon economy.
Tel. 0800 085 2005
www.carbontrust.co.uk

Energy Saving Trust

Advice on energy saving and links to sources for grants to help with insulation.
Tel. 0800 512 012
www.energysavingtrust.org.uk

Green Energy Works

Lots of advice on green electricity and examples of green energy being generated today. Information from the Green Party.
www.greenenergyworks.org.uk

National Energy Foundation

Offers people help throughout the UK to reduce their carbon emissions through the use of energy efficiency.
Tel. 01908 665555
www.nef.org.uk

Solar Trade Association

Promotes solar thermal in the UK.
Tel. 01908 442290
www.solar-trade.org.uk

INSULATION

Heat Project

Provides homeowners, residential landlords and private tenants with grant assisted loft and cavity wall insulation.
Tel. 0800 0934050
www.heatproject.co.uk

National Insulation Association

Offers information on how to improve heat-retention in your home.
Tel. 0845 163 6363
www.nationalinsulationassociation.org.uk

Warm Front

A government-funded initiative to provide grants for more energy-efficient homes.
Tel. 0800 316 2805
www.warmfront.co.uk

RECYCLING AND WASTE WEBSITES

Freecycle
Non-profit network for giving and receiving unwanted property for free.
www.freecycle.org

RecycleNow
Recycling information for the home and garden and other situations.
www.recyclenow.org.uk

Waste Watch
A UK environmental charity working to change the way people use the world's natural resources.
www.wastewatch.org.uk

WRAP (Waste & Resources Action Programme)
Advises individuals, businesses and local authorities on waste reduction and recycling, and helping to tackle climate change.
www.wrap.org.uk

WRAP also administer the Recycled Products Guide
The guide provides a national database of products made from recycled materials. Find products for your home, garden or office.
www.recycledproducts.org.uk

ECO-SUPPLIERS AND GREEN DIY ADVICE

Centre for Alternative Technology shop
www.cat.org.uk/shopping

Ecover
Produce biodegradable cleaning products that are available in many shops and supermarkets.
www.ecover.com

Green Building Store
Eco-friendly products and advice.
www.greenbuildingstore.co.uk

Sustainable Build
Eco-friendly building tips and advice.
www.sustainablebuild.co.uk

WWF's Earthly Goods shop
www.wwf.org.uk/shop

Chamois Eco Kitchens
Tel. 01902 864685
www.chamois.co.uk

Milestone Eco Design
Kitchens of recycled content.
Tel. 0845 456 7153
www.milestone.uk.net

The Curtain Exchange
Offers a secondhand curtain service.
www.thecurtainexchange.net

SAVING WATER
(See also Environment Agency page 186.)

Waterwise
A leading authority on water efficiency, which aims to help reduce water wastage in the UK and offers water-saving tips and advice.
Tel. 020 7344 1882
www.waterwise.org.uk

Water Guide
Provides information about the UK water industry.
www.water-guide.org.uk

RAINWATER AND GREYWATER SYSTEM SUPPLIERS

Freewater UK Ltd
Tel. 01522 720862
www.freewateruk.co.uk

ISS (Irrigation Systems and Service)
Tel. 01725 513880
www.solutionsforwater.co.uk

For DIY irrigation, and rainwater recycling equipment visit:
www.thewateringshop.co.uk

Ecoplay (CME Sanitary Systems)
Greywater management system which recycles bath and shower water and uses it to flush toilets.
Tel: 01709 770990
www.ecoplay-system.com

Cress Water Ltd
Specialises in the management of all the water resources on a site, including the design and installation of reed-bed systems.
Tel: 01884 849280
www.cresswater.co.uk

GREENER GARDENS

Garden Organic
Promotes organic gardening and has an online organic shop.
www.gardenorganic.org.uk

RHS (Royal Horticultural Society)
For advice on encouraging wildlife in your garden, as well as conservation and environmental guidelines.
www.rhs.org.uk

RSPB (Royal Society for the Preservation of Birds)
Guidance on wildlife gardening to encourage birds back into your garden.
www.rspb.org.uk

BUILDING MATERIALS – TRADE ASSOCIATIONS

British Cement Association
For information on the manufacture of cement, advice on working with cement including using it safely, as well as sustainability.
www.cementindustry.co.uk

BASA
The UKs only trade body representing the interests of industrial adhesives and sealants manufacturers.
www.basaonline.org

INDEX

A

Aggregate 184
Air-source heat pumps 137
Appliances 77, 78, 92–101

B

Bamboo 19, 42, 109, 162
Bark chips 165, 166
Bathrooms 80–85
Baths 80, 81
Bedding 108
Biofuel 130
Biomass 130
Biomass roofing 178
Black water 150, 184
Blinds 63, 88
Boilers 140–143
Bricks 16, 22–25, 161, 165
British Fenestration Rating
    Council (BFRC) 49

C

Carbon dioxide 4, 8–9, 119
Carbon emissions 184
Carbon footprint 8–9,
    116–117, 184
Carpets 41, 109–110
Caulking 62, 184
Cavity wall insulation 65–66
Cellulose insulation 57, 58,
    184
Cement 12, 16, 22, 28–31, 185
Cement plaster 184
Central heating 132
Chemicals, toxic 33–34, 37–40
Clay 177, 184
Cleaning products 79, 81, 85

Climate change 4, 8, 184
Coal 115, 116
Cob building 24
Coir 42
Combination boilers 141
Compact Fluorescent Lamp
    bulbs (CFLs) 89–90, 184
Composting 27, 75, 76, 77,
    159
Computers 106
Concrete 28, 165, 166, 167,
    177
Condensing boilers 140–141
Convection 184
Coppiced woodlands 162
Cork 41, 42, 57
Cotton 108
Curtains 63, 88

D

Daylight tubes 86–87
Decking 167–168
Dishwashers 76, 99
Doors 50–52
Double glazing 46–47,
    48, 60–62
Drainage boxes 184
Draught-proofing 52, 62
Drives 164–168

E

Earth blocks 24
Electrical equipment 102–106
    see also Appliances
Electricity, green 119,
    120–127
Energy
    controlling usage 116–117

reserves 114–119
sustainable 115, 116,
    117, 120–127
Energy Saving Recommended
    models 94–95, 99, 100,
    101, 105, 140
Energy Saving Trust 9, 90,
    93, 117
EU Energy Labels 93–94, 101

F

Fabrics 108–109
Fencing 161–163, 164
Fertilisers 158, 160
Fibreglass 57, 58
Finishing touches 107–111
Fires 129
Flax-based insulation 57, 58
Floors 41–42, 64–65, 74, 83
Foam insulation 57, 58
Food 79
Forest Stewardship Council
    (FSC) 18, 20–21
Fossil fuels 114–116, 184
Freezers 95, 100–101
Fridges 94, 95, 100–101
Furniture 110–111, 169–170

G

Gadgets 102–106
Games consoles 106
Gardens 157–175
    accessories for 169–170
    rooftop 179–183
    watering 173–175
Gas 115, 116
Geothermal heat pumps
    137–139

Glass 43, 46–47, 51, 75, 184
Glasstex 110
Global warming 184
Glues 17, 37–40
Granite 165
Grants 55, 123, 126, 131, 136, 139
Gravel 165, 166
Green roofs 179–183, 185
Greenhouse gases 184
Grey water 150–153, 172, 184
Ground-source heat pumps 137–139

H

Hammocks 169
Heat loss, preventing 51–52
Heat pumps 137–139
Heating 128–143, 185
Hedging 161, 163–164
Hemp-based insulation 55, 56, 58
Household Waste Recycling Centres (HWRC) 27
Hurdles 162

I

Incandescent bulbs 89–90
Insulation 47, 48, 50, 52–69, 179, 184
International Energy Agency (IEA) 86
Irrigation systems 174–175, 181

J

Jute 42

K

Kitchens 73–79

L

Lagging 68–69, 81
Landfill sites 26
Lawnmowers 160, 172
Lawns 171–172
Light bulbs 88, 89–91, 184
Light Emitting Diodes (LEDs) 91, 184
Light tubes 86–87, 185
Lighting 83, 85, 86–91, 170, 184, 185
Lime mortar 30–31, 32
Lime plaster 32, 185
Linoleum, natural 42
Living roofs 179–183, 185
Loft insulation 64
Loos 81, 82
Low Carbon Buildings Programme 123, 126, 131, 136, 139
Low-emissivity coatings 50, 51, 60–61, 185

M

Marble 165
Mattresses 109
MDF 19, 185
Megaflow system 141
Metal 43, 111
Microgeneration 185
Microwaves 76, 101
Mortar 28, 30–31, 32, 185

N

Noise pollution 60, 164
Nuclear energy 116, 118

O

Oil 115
Ovens 101

P

Paint 17, 33–36
Paper, recycling 75
Patios 164–168
Paving 164–168
Peat 160
Petrochemicals 33–34, 185
Photovoltaic (PV) solar power 121–124, 134, 185
Pipe insulation 68–69, 81
Planning permission 61, 122, 125, 135
Plaster 17, 32, 184, 185
Plastic 75, 111, 169
Pointing 185
Programme for the Endorsement of Forest Certification (PEFC) 18, 20

R

Radiation 185
Radios 106
Rainfall 145
Rainwater harvesting 146–149, 172, 185
Reclamation yards 19, 22, 43, 84
Recycled materials 43–44
Recycling 27, 36, 75, 79, 83, 157, 159
Render 66–67
Renewable energy 185
Renewables Obligation 119
Roofs 176–183
    green 179–183
    insulation 64, 179
Rubber tiles 44
Rubbish 26–27, 100
    see also Recycling
Rugs 109–110

S

Sealants 17, 37–40
Secondary glazing 60
SEDBUK boiler efficiency
    table 143
Set-top boxes 105
Shingled roofs 178
Showers 80, 82
Shutters 62, 63
Slates 177
Smart meters 118, 185
Soft furnishings 108–110
Solar energy 121–124
Solar water heating 134–136
Solid wall insulation 66–67
Sound proofing 60, 164
Standby 102, 103
Stone 12, 17, 24, 165, 166, 167
Storage in kitchens 78
Storage tanks 140
Stoves, wood-burning
    130–133
Straw bale houses 25

T

Tableware 111
Tank insulation 68–69
Taps 81, 83
Tarmac 167

Televisions 104–105
Thatched roofs 178
Tiles 17, 43–44
Timber see Wood
Toilets 81, 82
Tumble driers 94, 97, 98
Turf 171, 172

U

Units, kitchen 74
UPVC 13, 48, 61

V

Varnish 17
Vegetable gardens 160
Ventilation 85
Volatile organic compounds
    (VOCs) 33–34, 37, 38–40, 185

W

Walls
    brick 23, 161
    coverings 110
    garden 161, 164
    insulation 65–67, 83
    wood 23–24
Washing machines 94, 96, 98
Waste 26–27, 100

Water 144–153
    black 150, 184
    grey 150–153, 172
    heating 134–136, 140–143
    rainwater harvesting
        146–149, 172, 185
    saving 80–81, 84
    surface run-off 166
    water meters 145
    watering the garden
        173–175
Weatherstripping 52, 62, 185
Wildlife gardens 157, 158, 163
Wind power 124–127, 185
Windows 45–49, 85, 88, 185
    insulating 60–63
    Window Energy ratings 49
Wood 12, 16, 18–21
    decking 167–168
    doors 50
    fencing 161–162
    flooring 41
    furniture 110–111, 169, 170
    kitchen units 74
    roofs 178
    walls 23–24
    windows 48, 61
Wood-fired heating 129–134
Wool 41, 108, 109
    insulation 55, 56, 58
Worktops 74

ACKNOWLEDGEMENTS

Thanks to Cresta Norris, Nina Sharman, Katie Hewett, Caroline King and everyone at Collins & Brown who has contributed to the research and production of this book. Special thanks to Matt Sexton at B&Q for his advice on eco paints, Tim Ashton at Hunters Architects, Dale Vince at Ecotricity, Rupert Little and Peter Ainsworth.